publishing for success

a practical guide

ANNE TANNAHILL

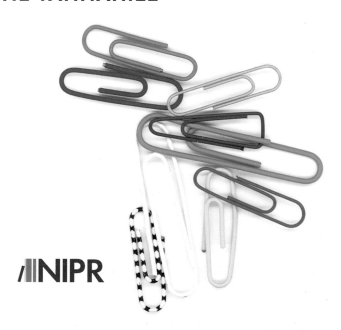

/IINIPR

Imprint page

The imprint page (also called the title page verso) always appears on a left-hand page, usually immediately after the title page; it occasionally appears on the last page of heavily illustrated books, particularly those for children. It should contain the following **essential** information: the year of first and any subsequent publication; the name and address of the publisher; a copyright line beginning with the copyright symbol © and giving the copyright holder's name and date of first publication; the International Standard Book Number (ISBN); and the printer's name and address. It **may** also contain: a general notice about copyright such as 'All rights reserved'; Cataloguing-in-Publication (CIP) data (often using a form of words such as 'A catalogue record for this book is available from the British Library'); the name(s) and, if required, the logo(s) of sponsors; the publisher's logo and/or website address; the name(s) of the designer and/or typesetter; and information about the typeface and paper used in the book. In addition, the dedication and/or acknowledgements are sometimes presented on the imprint page if space is tight in the rest of the book.

LOTTERY FUNDED

First published in 2008 by
Northern Ireland Publications Resource
Linen Hall Library
17 Donegall Square North
Belfast BT1 5GB
with the assistance of
Awards for All and W & G Baird Ltd

© Northern Ireland Publications Resource, 2008

All rights reserved

Designed and typeset by Dunbar Design, Holywood, County Down

Printed by W & G Baird Ltd, Antrim, County Antrim

A CIP catalogue record for this book is available from the British Library

ISBN 978-0-9557419-0-6

www.nibooks.org

Contents

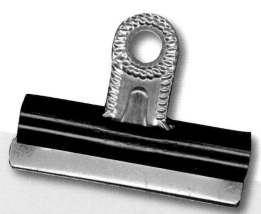

WRITING ◉ ULSTER NO 5 1998

THE UNIVERSITY OF ULSTER

Vere Foster English Gentleman, Irish Champion 1819–1900 BRENDAN COLGAN FOUNTAIN PUBLISHING

NEW UPDATED EDITION A History of ULSTER · JONATHAN BARDON THE · BLACK · STAFF

Sir Roger Casement's HEART of DARKNESS THE 1911 DOCUMENTS

THE LAKE WITHOUT A NAME MICHAEL LONGLEY

A CENSUS OF IRELAND CIRCA 1659 WITH ESSENTIAL MATERIALS from the POLL MONEY ORDINANCES 1660–1661 EDITED BY SÉAMUS PENDER WITH A NEW INTRODUCTION BY WILLIAM J SMYTH

Cholvim Chille *Elegy for Columba* PL HENRY colme

The Birth of the TITANIC MICHAEL McCAUGHAN

Springhill AN OLD ULSTER HOUSE MINA LENOX-CONYNGHAM

DOWN CATHEDRAL The Church of Saint Patrick of Down FREDERICK RANKIN

The Image of Ireland

STRANGFORD LOUGH An archaeological survey of the maritime cultural landscape THOMAS McERLEAN ROSEMARY McCONKEY WES FORSYTHE THE · BLACK · STAFF

BELFAST A CENTURY JONATHAN BARDON

The Northern Ireland Publications Resource (NIPR) was established with the task of identifying, acquiring, cataloguing and preserving every title published in Northern Ireland since January 2000. Its aim is to supplement the role of legal deposit and to ensure that copies are held in Northern Ireland libraries for future generations of readers. NIPR relies on the generosity of the local publishing community, and it is a pleasure to record that thanks to the willing participation of publishers both large and small across Northern Ireland more than 4,200 titles have been collected. Every week sees more and more added to the database as publishers realise the value of having their titles preserved and made known throughout the world of books.

In 2003 with the generous support of Royal Mail a competition was organised to choose and reward the best local history publication since 2000. More than 160 publications were entered, covering a huge breadth of topics and ranging from short pamphlets on townland history to large-scale works of solid scholarship.

However, it was apparent to the team of judges that many publications, although they had a good story to tell, displayed poor standards of design and production and fell far short of what, with a bit of knowledge and experience, they could have been. NIPR came to see that as well as collecting published titles it had a role to play in promoting good practice in publishing and in encouraging publishers to set their sights higher. To this end a seminar on good practice in publishing was held in September 2006 which proved an enormous success. NIPR was asked to provide more guidance and so it was decided to publish this guide.

The Board was delighted when Anne Tannahill agreed to manage the project and write the body of the text. Anne was for many years managing director of Blackstaff Press, which has an international reputation for the quality of its publications. No one is better fitted than she to offer practical guidance in the art and science of publishing within a provincial context. Anyone who sets out to publish a book giving direction on good practice had better make sure that they stick to their own precepts and so the Board was also very pleased to secure the services of the award-winning designer Wendy Dunbar.

In order to ensure that the guide will reach as wide a readership as possible NIPR resolved that it should be distributed freely to whomever might find it helpful. That has been made possible thanks to the generous sponsorship of W & G Baird and funding from Awards for All.

Monica McErlane, the NIPR manager, has compiled the Appendices, which contain many useful links to other individuals and organisations. These will be kept up to date on the NIPR website www.nibooks.org.

It is NIPR's wish that this guide will encourage individuals and groups to publish and reach the highest standards in design, production and distribution.

WESLEY McCANN
CHAIR, NIPR BOARD

Acknowledgements

This book is the brainchild of Wesley McCann of NIPR. When he approached me with the idea of writing a practical publishing guide for NIPR I felt both flattered and a little daunted by the task ahead. I needn't have worried: the unfailing enthusiasm and support shown by him and Monica McErlane throughout the writing process made my task not only easier, but far more pleasurable than I could have anticipated. Monica, who was responsible for compiling the useful information contained in the Appendices, also answered my numerous queries promptly and cheerfully. I am extremely grateful to them both.

I am also indebted to Hilary Bell whose comments on the editing section were invaluable; to Seamus Cashman, who made useful suggestions on an early draft; to Wendy Dunbar, whose technical knowledge kept me straight on matters of design and production; and to Roger Dixon and Fintan Mullan for their helpful perusal of the script. Thanks are also due for specific advice readily given by Robin Gourley of Eason Ireland, Alyson Wilson of Waterstone's and my former colleagues at Blackstaff Press. As well as making a telling contribution to the sections on sales and marketing, Brian Tannahill also gave me constructive feedback on each piece of writing as it emerged. My thanks to him, as always.

This project was funded by Awards for All and sponsored by W & G Baird; gratitude is due to both bodies for their far-sighted generosity.

ANNE TANNAHILL

Introduction

At its best, publishing is one of the most absorbing, challenging and rewarding pursuits imaginable. At its worst, it is frustrating, exhausting and financially hazardous.

But what does a publisher actually do? A useful comparison might be the direction of a stage play. The core creative work may already have been done by the playwright but to present the play to the audience the director needs to recruit and orchestrate another group of people – the actors, obviously, but also set and costume designers, sound and lighting engineers, musicians perhaps, and so on.

With publishing, the core creative work is the original text and/or illustrations that make up the proposed book. The publisher's job is to transform this basic material into multiple copies of a finished, marketable book. To do this, he or she has to co-ordinate the following tasks: editing and proofing; design; typesetting; printing and binding; publicity and sales; warehousing and distribution; and, of course, accounting. There will most likely also be legal issues to be considered. A large commercial publisher will have sizeable departments devoted to each of these activities; a small one will rely on far fewer people, perhaps only one. Whatever the setup, the publishing process is broadly the same.

> The aim of this little guide is ... to provide a clear outline of the publishing process, with friendly, practical advice about sensible paths to follow and common pitfalls to avoid.

To describe each stage in depth would fill a small library of specialist books. The aim of this little guide is more modest: to provide a clear outline of the publishing process, with friendly, practical advice about sensible paths to follow and common pitfalls to avoid.

The decision to become a publisher may spring from any number of motives. You or your group may have the urge to record the history of an individual life, or a family, a community or an area. Or perhaps there is a particular enthusiasm you want to share, or a cause you want to champion. You may even hope that publishing is an easy way to make a lot of money very quickly.

Often, the trigger is a feeling of frustration because commercial publishers have rejected a proposed book that you believe in, whether written by yourself or someone else. If this is the case, it's worth stopping for a moment and wondering why this has happened. It's true that commercial publishers can and do make mistakes in their selection

Vanity publishing

The term 'vanity publishing' is sometimes mistakenly applied to self-publishing, where individuals publish books at their own expense and derive income from sales. By and large, vanity publishers charge a fee (often a large one) for converting a text into a quantity of printed books which are then delivered to the author, who is responsible for any marketing and distribution. Frequently the vanity publisher will undertake little or nothing in the way of editorial improvements or focused design, and the result is an unattractive, all-but-unsellable product. No author royalties are payable and all the production costs, plus of course a profit for the vanity publisher, are payable by the author who may or may not recoup some of the outlay through sales income.

processes, but most of them are actively looking out for promising new work amongst the huge numbers of proposals they receive. They are experienced in separating the wheat from the chaff and you should consider what it was about your work that led to the decision to reject it. Hard though it might be to accept, the most common reason for turning down a proposed book is that it is badly written and/or poorly organised. Other factors might be that the subject doesn't suit a particular publisher's list, or that it's felt to be unfashionable or dated or too obscure, or that there is a current glut of such books.

On the other hand, it may merely be that your proposed book is thought unlikely to sell well enough outside a limited region or interest group to cover the considerable production costs faced by a publisher with a large establishment. This can be your opportunity – with lower financial overheads and a more intimate and up-to-date knowledge of the likely readership, many so-called 'amateur' publications have performed exceptionally well.

If you decide to publish your own work (i.e. self-publish) you will need to develop something of a split personality: on the one hand that of the enthusiastic creative writer and on the other that of the cooler, more analytical and critical publisher. This is not an easy feat and (without floundering in a morass of too many opinions) it's a good idea to run your work past people whose opinion you respect – *not* those you think will give you an ego-boosting report regardless of quality.

One area where self-publishers often come into their own is in marketing, especially publicity and promotion. Here their eager belief in their own work and their passion for the subject can become powerful sales tools, enabling them to persuade journalists that their book will make an interesting feature or to coax booksellers into giving it a more prominent display.

The guidelines, tips and pointers in the following chapters should not be interpreted as a set of rigid rules and conventions. Like any creative or business process, publishing is constantly changing and being modified by new ideas, and you may well devise an original way of tackling a task that suits you better. But we hope that *Publishing for Success* will give your venture into publishing a firm basis and will save you from having to reinvent numerous wheels.

Above all, we hope that it will smooth your way to the exciting moment when you hold the first copy of your book in your hand and know that it is as well edited, designed and printed as you could possibly have made it. Just as importantly, you'll be confident that your forward planning on publicity, sales and distribution means that copies of the book will soon be in the hands of hundreds, perhaps thousands, of delighted readers.

Shaping the project

Put simply, publishing is a process that turns an idea into a physical reality and makes it available to others in the form of a finished book. As a publisher, your first task in this process is to pin down the intangible idea and give it a workable shape.

If you are starting from scratch and think you could create an attractive book from an idea of your own, you have the choice of researching and writing it yourself, or of commissioning someone else to do it. On the other hand, you may know of an already existing work, again by yourself or by someone else, that seems worthy of publication.

When commissioning a book, it can be quite difficult to identify the best writer for the job. People who can talk knowledgeably about a subject don't always have the skill or discipline to write well about it. For this reason, you should be careful not to commit yourself to a writer until you have seen a sizeable example of his or her work, in the form of a detailed outline of the proposed book and two or three sample chapters. If it is an illustrated book, you should also ensure that your proposed author not only knows how to go about finding appropriate illustrations or photographs but also where and how to obtain any necessary copyright or reproduction permissions.

With a work that already exists, you should satisfy yourself that it is of a high enough standard to warrant the considerable time, effort and money you are going to expend on publishing it. If you feel that it needs major amendments, deletions or additions, make sure that the writer is willing to co-operate with you before you make a hard commitment, and certainly before signature of the publisher/author agreement. Remember that if you are self-publishing your own book it's vital to show your work at an early stage to someone you are confident will give you an informed and above all *honest* opinion.

It's important to give some thought to the category of the proposed book. Will it fit into the immensely wide range of non-fiction, which includes everything from history, art, and personal memoir to poetry and sport, or is it a novel or collection of short stories that falls into the fiction category? The question of category is important because it will influence your decisions about the format of the book (what it will look like), its target readership (who's going to be interested enough to buy it) and your marketing strategy (how you're going to sell and distribute it).

It's also worth doing a bit of preliminary research to establish whether there is room in the market for your proposed book. It may be that a similar book is currently in print and has soaked up most of your potential buyers or, conversely, it may have made them eager for more books on the subject. Or it could be that your target readers are scattered over a wider geographical area than you are able to reach effectively or economically – for instance, if your local market is north Antrim and your book is about building techniques in desert conditions, you are defeated before you begin unless you can access a very specialised list of potential buyers and establish how many of them will actually buy it at a price that makes commercial sense for you.

Obtaining some idea of the size of the market for the proposed book is essential if you are to make sensible decisions about, for instance, how many copies to order from the printer (the print run). The market may be very small, for example friends and family members in the case of a personal memoir, or quite large, with a local topic like the *Titanic* that generates worldwide interest. The likelihood is somewhere in between, but never forget that publishing is a notoriously unpredictable business and that, even with an apparently sure-fire subject, success is far from guaranteed. Having a confidential word with a trusted bookseller can give you a better idea about the sales potential of your book but it's worth remembering that even the most experienced bookseller can be mistaken, especially with an unusual subject that doesn't yet have a track record.

> ' It's also worth doing a bit of preliminary research to establish whether there is room in the market for your proposed book. '

To help you focus on the ideal format for your book, you should think hard about your target readers. Questions about whether it should be presented as a handsome coffee-table hardback or a simple paperback, or whether it should be illustrated lavishly, modestly or not at all, or if there will be tables, notes or an index, will all depend on the target readers' expectations and spending power. Are they people who aren't regular book-buyers but who will be interested in, say, a history of their school or church, provided it's not too expensive? Or are they likely to be discriminating readers who expect high standards of writing and production quality, and are prepared to pay for them?

If illustrations and photographs are to be an important element in your book, you need to be confident that enough strong, reproducible images exist to make an attractive book – and that they have not lost their impact by frequent publication elsewhere. Make sure that they are both interesting and informative and can be made more so by well-researched and well-written captions. Find out whether it will be complicated or relatively straightforward to obtain permission to reproduce them in your book, and whether any requested permission fees are within your budget.

Your publicity and marketing plans will be more effective if you try to predict things like the likely balance among your target readers of, for example, gender and age. If your subject has a specialist appeal, say steam trains, you'll be wasting your money by promoting the book in a trendy lifestyle magazine. Instead, you'd do better to concentrate your efforts on enthusiast magazines and perhaps look into the feasibility of taking a stall at a vintage vehicle rally. Having a clear idea of the target readership for your book will also be a key factor in helping you with the sensitive task of setting its retail price. Other factors will include your production and sales costs, the level of discounts demanded by booksellers and other outlets, competition from similar books – you can get a good idea of this by browsing in a bookshop – and your desired profit.

Try to settle on a title for your book as early in the process as you can. Apart from needing it for advance information to the book trade, you'll find that a well thought-out title, plus perhaps a subtitle, will help to give the book a sharper focus during the editing and design processes. Choosing a title that both reflects the contents of the book and helps it to sell can be quite difficult, especially where there are a number of people to satisfy. It's an inexact science and as such can't be governed by simple rules, but there are a few things to keep in mind. For non-fiction, the main title should indicate what the book is about. Generally, it's better to have a prosaic title like *Portrush: An Illustrated History* than a less informative one like *Sandcastles and Donkey-rides*, which, although more evocative, could be about any seaside town. If you feel strongly that you'd like an evocative main title, make sure that you add a subtitle which fills in the missing information, e.g. *Sandcastles and Donkey-rides: An Illustrated History of Portrush.* For fiction or poetry, titles can be as fanciful as you like as long as you add 'A novel' or 'Poems' to the front cover design. And while there's no law that says you can't use a title that's been used before, it's obviously a bad idea to use the title of a well-known book or one that has been recently published – you can ask a librarian or bookseller to run a check for you.

Setting time aside to reflect calmly about these aspects of the project before you plunge into the hurly-burly of the production process may seem frustrating when you are full of enthusiasm and raring to go. You will find, however, that it has been time well spent, and that it will help to give you some useful points of reference when you are faced with the scores of large and small decisions that publishing will throw at you on a daily basis.

Financial management

In many ways, financial management is the same for publishing as for any other business. A budget is worked out showing likely expenditure on production and marketing alongside likely income from sales. The point at which the amount of expenditure equals the amount of income is the break-even point. The positive balance, if any, between expenditure and income is the profit and the negative balance, if any, between expenditure and income is the loss.

This all seems simple enough. However, the fact is that publishing is widely regarded as a particularly difficult and risky business. Why should this be?

The major cause of risk is the volatility of the book market and the impossibility of predicting in advance which books will sell well and which won't. This basic problem in turn generates a whole set of sub-problems, including the nerve-racking gamble of deciding a print-run quantity in the absence of sufficient sales information. In addition, the book-trade practice of returning unsold books means that money that has been recorded as sales income can suddenly become money that has to be paid back.

Cash flow is difficult in other ways. For instance, there is a built-in lag of two or three months (or even longer) between the publisher having to pay for the production and marketing of books and receiving the sales income from them. Many commercial publishers cover this lag by borrowing, with bank interest adding yet another expenditure item to the profit and loss account. Others delay paying creditors for as long as possible; while this tactic is sometimes unavoidable, it shouldn't be used too often – in addition to damaging the publisher's credibility, it will make disgruntled suppliers less than co-operative if, say, a fast reprint is needed. With cash flow, it's useful to remember the old business adage: 'Turnover is vanity, profit is sanity, cash is reality.'

This all sounds pretty gloomy, but it is possible for small publishers as well as large ones to make a profit in spite of the difficulties. It is important, however, to realise that publishing is not a sure-fire method of making money fast. Going into a

> Turnover is vanity, profit is sanity, cash is reality.

publishing project with your eyes wide open is much more sensible and I hope that this chapter will help you to do just that.

Preparing the budget

Before you commit yourself to publishing a book, and certainly before you have committed yourself to any expenditure, it is wise to draw up a simple budget of likely expenditure and income, including as many items as you can think of. The sample budget on the next page will give you the main item headings – remember that while some of them may not apply to your project, you may need to include other items that are not listed here.

Production costs

The sample budget includes editing, proofing and design under both internal and external costs because these are tasks you may decide either to undertake yourself or to farm out to a professional editor or designer. If you are doing them yourself, it is your choice whether or not to include them as cost items in the budget – you may be content to regard your work as 'free' at this stage in the hope that you will get your reward later in the form of a larger profit. If you are using a professional editor or designer, ask for a written estimate before you place the job and before you compile the budget.

> **it is essential to shop around before you commit to any one printer**

If you are paying the author a fixed fee or an advance on royalties, you should enter the amount under 'external production costs'. The payment of advance royalties is optional; it is based on predicted earnings from the sale of books and, unless the author is very insistent, it is prudent not to pay any royalties until you have a better idea of how sales have gone. These royalties (i.e. those not paid in advance) should be entered further down the budget as a deduction from 'estimated sales income'.

You will see 'administration & overheads' as an internal cost item in the sample budget. This is intended to cover such costs as phone calls, postage stamps, stationery etc, as well as an appropriate portion of household expenses like heat and light. Again, it is your choice how much of these expenses to include in the budget, as long as you bear in mind that they are actual costs and that by not including them you are unrealistically inflating your profit line.

As 'printing & binding' will be one of the major production costs, it is essential to shop around before you commit to any one printer. Seek advice on economical formats etc before preparing a specification. Send

TITLE

Print run:
Retail price:

Production costs
Internal production costs

Editing*	£00.00
Proofing*	£00.00
Design*	£00.00
Administration & overheads	£00.00

External production costs

Editing *	£00.00
Proofing*	£00.00
Design*	£00.00
Typesetting	£00.00
Advance royalties (if any)	£00.00
Permissions	£00.00
Photography/Illustrations	£00.00
Printing & binding	£00.00

Sales costs

Publicity inc. launch costs	£00.00
Sales material	£00.00
Postage & packing	£00.00
Warehousing	£00.00
Travel	£00.00

Total estimated production and sales costs £00.00

less estimated sales income ...

Gross units (qty)[1]	0000
Retail price	£00.00
Gross sales income	£00.00
less average discount @ 45 %[2]	(£00.00)

Net invoice value £00.00

less ongoing author royalties (£00.00)

Total estimated sales income £00.00

Total estimated production and sales costs £00.00
less total estimated sales income (£00.00)

Estimated profit/(loss) £00.00/(£00.00)

*Asterisked items may be treated as internal or external costs – see p 7.

[1] Gross units = quantity printed less free copies

[2] Average discount for guidance only – may vary

your printing specification (see sample on next page) to three experienced book printers, requesting estimates and samples of books they have printed for other publishers. The lowest estimate needn't necessarily be the best for your purposes – satisfy yourself that your chosen printer has the expertise and equipment to produce your books to a satisfactory standard and deliver them within an acceptable time.

If you hope to reproduce copyright material in your book – poems, songs, extracts, music, photographs, paintings etc – it's worthwhile making some preliminary enquiries about likely permission costs before finalising the budget. In some cases, for example with extracts from the work of famous writers still in copyright, the requested fees may give you such a shock that you have to rethink your use of such material.

> ❝ with extracts from the work of famous writers still in copyright, the requested fees may give you such a shock that you have to rethink ❞

Sales costs

You should include under 'sales costs' all expenditure incurred in actually selling the book, including cost of travel when hunting for orders and delivering books, phone calls to the media, design and printing costs for sales material, and launch costs (printing and posting invitations, venue hire, refreshments etc). Also include distribution costs like postage, packing and any warehouse costs like rent, heating etc.

Estimated sales income

Once you have a total for your production and sales costs, work out your estimated sales income from copies available for sale. Base this on the quantity of copies printed, less the quantity you will be giving away free to the author, the media, legal deposit etc. Multiply the retail price by this quantity to calculate 'gross sales income' and deduct an average trade discount (45 per cent as a rule of thumb) to work out 'net invoice value'. From this amount you should then deduct an estimated amount for

How many copies should I print?

Getting the print run right is extremely difficult, even for experienced publishers. The most common mistake with new publishers is to order too many copies because they overestimate the number of people who will not only be interested in their projected book but will be prepared to search it out and buy it. Matters are made worse when the publishers realise that the cost of printing each copy (the unit cost) decreases as the print quantity increases. This can seem like an easy way to enhance the profit, but don't forget that the *total* printing bill will be higher, and that it will be a false economy unless you can sell all the extra books. The opposite mistake, of ordering too few copies, can create its own problems but, provided a sensible budget is in place, is far less damaging financially.

NIPR GUIDE FOR PUBLISHERS (working title)

Extent	80 pages
of which	80 pp in full colour
	Allow for bleed
Format	240 x 165 mm
Illustrations	Colour throughout
Paper	150 gsm Satimatt
Binding (hb/pb)	sewn paperback
Cover (full colour)	300 gsm silk two-sided board
	matt lamination
Quantity	3,000 run on
Delivery of print-ready copy	mid-January 2008
Publication date	March 2008

NOTE

The above sample specification, which is roughly based on this book, shows the main elements you need to cover when requesting an estimate from a printer (you should seek estimates from at least three printers). Before finalising your specification, have a word with one or two printers and ask to see samples of books they have printed – they will be able to advise you on such matters as economical formats and paper quality. If necessary, add delivery instructions – how you would like the books packed, for instance, and your preferred delivery address.

author royalties (see note above on advance royalties) to arrive at the 'total estimated sales income'.

The bottom line

Now deduct the 'total estimated sales income' from the 'total estimated production and sales costs'. All being well, the result will be a positive amount; this is your estimated profit. If it is a negative amount – i.e. if expenditure is greater than income – this is your estimated loss or shortfall.

Tweaking the budget

If you don't like how the bottom line has turned out, have another look at the budget and see if there's any way you can improve it by reducing costs and/or increasing estimated sales income.

To reduce costs, you could settle for a less ambitious format, thereby reducing spending on printing and other items, or you could print fewer copies (but remember this will both increase the unit cost and leave you with fewer copies to sell). Or you might decide that rather than paying a professional editor or designer you will undertake such tasks yourself. It might well be possible to persuade the author not to take an advance on royalties but to wait for an agreed time after publication (this can also avoid the problem of a book not 'earning out' its advance – quite a frequent occurrence). Or, as mentioned above, you might be able to cut back on the amount of copyright material you had intended to use.

To improve sales income, consider increasing the retail price (but don't forget that this will make the book harder to sell), or printing more copies (always remembering that it will need extra cost and effort to sell them). You could also try to find ways of lowering the average discount by, for example, concentrating on direct sales to the public rather than relying on the book trade.

You can create extra income via funding from other bodies – this might be anything from a Lottery grant to a donation from a local business. Sometimes it's easier to get funding in kind rather than cash, for example by persuading a hotel that it makes sense to provide a free room, or even wine, for your book launch because of the extra bar and restaurant trade they'll get from your guests.

Another way to generate income is by selling advertising space in your book. This used to be quite common, but is rarely seen nowadays. However, there's no reason why you shouldn't do it,

Pricing

Deciding on an effective retail price is quite a complex matter. Too expensive, and you make it unattractive to customers. Too cheap, and your sales income takes a hammering.

However, what is too expensive for one market may be quite acceptable to another. If your book is specialised and you have an accurate idea of the number of likely customers *and* how to contact them, you will be able to set a much higher price than if you are publishing a book that has wider appeal and has to compete against similar cheaply priced books. Do some research before you set the retail price. Go into a bookshop and see how different types of books are priced – average retail prices may be quite a bit lower than you were planning for your book, or they may be higher. Either way, you may need to rethink.

provided the author doesn't object and you don't mind the considerable extra work of selling advertising space, negotiating rates, agreeing and organising the text and design of the advertisements, and – not least – invoicing, statementing and chasing the advertisers for payment.

Really, tweaking the budget is all a matter of juggling the different items and trying various combinations of 'what if?'. (If you can access a software programme like Microsoft Office Excel, you'll find a spreadsheet very handy for this operation.) Even the most detailed budget can only give an estimate of how things might work out in reality, but the exercise of preparing one is an essential discipline that means you are at least forewarned and forearmed against the most common publishing pitfalls.

To summarise, financial management needn't be too difficult provided you apply plenty of common sense and take time to consider the pros and cons before you commit yourself to any sizeable expenditure. The production and sales aspects of publishing are so interesting and labour-intensive that it's all too easy to take your eye off the financial ball. That's why a reasonably realistic budget that you can refer to as you go along is such an asset, and well worth the effort it has taken to prepare it.

It may seem overly cautious to have to stop and consider legal matters so early in the publishing process, especially when you are only intending to publish on a small scale. However, publishing on any level involves tackling a number of legal concerns and it is as well to have a clear idea of what the main ones are. Offences such as infringement of copyright, libel and plagiarism can land you in court, with serious results for your financial, not to mention emotional, wellbeing. Bear in mind that this chapter can only skim the surface of what is a notoriously complex field of law and that if you are in any doubt about a particular matter you may need to seek professional legal advice.

Copyright

In simple terms, copyright is a property right that attaches to an original work of art: such work can be literary, visual (for example illustrations and photographs), dramatic or musical. It arises automatically when a work is created in permanent form, whether in writing or by visual, audio or electronic means. (Contrary to some mistaken beliefs, copyright does not require some sort of formal registration, nor has it anything to do with the legal deposit or ISBN systems.) In general, copyright belongs to the creators of works during their lifetime and, in the UK and Ireland, to their estates until seventy years from the year in which they died.

As a publisher, you will be concerned with two aspects of copyright: the copyright of the book you are publishing (usually the author's copyright) and the copyright of work by other people that the author and you wish to reproduce in your book, and for which you will require permission.

With author copyright, what usually happens in a publishing agreement is that the copyright holder, e.g. the author or the author's estate, exclusively licenses the publisher to reproduce his or her work in a specified way, for example in a certain territory and for a certain length of time. Such agreements usually provide that, if the work goes and remains out of print for a specified time, the rights revert to the author.

It's worth bearing in mind that if you have obtained from an author the right to publish a book previously published by another publisher, you cannot simply reproduce a facsimile of the original book unless more than twenty-five years have passed since its first publication. This is because publishers possess rights in such elements as the design and typesetting of their books. However, you may be able to negotiate an arrangement that suits both publishers; as always with legal matters, make sure that you keep records of all correspondence, conversations and agreements.

If a proposed book contains work that is the copyright of persons other than the author, it will in most cases be essential to obtain and possibly pay for permission to use it.

Permissions

Plagiarism

Put simply, plagiarism is using the creative work of another person without acknowledgement and as if it were your own – stealing, in other words. If the work used is in the public domain (for example, if the creator has been dead for more than seventy years) plagiarism is not necessarily an infringement of copyright, but it should always be avoided as both unethical and unprofessional. Much depends on the author's honesty, but if an alert editor spots an instance of plagiarism, he or she should insist that either the passage be deleted or that it be kept only if written permission is obtained and a proper acknowledgement made.

Unless a work is in the public domain, for example where copyright has expired because the author has been dead for over seventy years, written permission to reproduce any part of it is a legal requirement. An exception is where a quoted passage could be regarded as 'non-substantial', e.g. very short. However, there are no hard-and-fast rules about these exceptional circumstances, sometimes referred to as 'fair dealing' – a 100-word extract from a prose work might pass the test, whereas a poem of the same length would not. If there is any doubt, it is better to be safe than sorry and to seek permission. In any case, in-copyright work must never be used without proper acknowledgement. Even where the work is not in copyright, you should give credit where credit is due – it is always unethical to present the work of someone else as if it were your own.

Obtaining permission for the right to reproduce copyright work is in theory the responsibility of the author; in practice the task is sometimes undertaken by the publisher. In either case, it is in the publisher's interest to ensure that it has been carefully and properly carried out, with all relevant correspondence and memos of phone conversations and meetings efficiently filed. Payment of any permission fees is also the author's responsibility; this is sometimes handled by an arrangement whereby the publisher pays the copyright holders and reduces the amount of royalties the author receives.

Whether author or publisher, the person handling permissions should write to the copyright holder or his or her publisher or agent enclosing a photocopy of the relevant extract, illustration, photograph etc and requesting written permission to reproduce it in the forthcoming book, for which details (title, author, retail price, print run and publication date) should also be given. As a publisher will generally have the right to negotiate permissions on behalf of an author provided the book is still in print, it is usually simpler to write to the publisher in the first instance. You may be lucky and be granted written permission free of charge, provided the copyright holder is properly acknowledged (perhaps using a precise specified form of words) and that you send a copy of the book upon publication. On the other hand, you will probably be asked to pay a permission fee and, in the case of, say, a museum which holds a painting or photograph you want

> ' Don't on any account go ahead and use the material in the hope that you won't get caught out '

to use, a reproduction fee as well. This may be considerably more than you had expected, particularly in the case of famous writers or artists. In this case you can try to negotiate a lower fee or, as a last resort, decide not to use the material at all. Don't on any account go ahead and use the material in the hope that you won't get caught out – it could turn out to be an expensive move, damaging both to your credibility and your bank balance.

Acknowledgements

Legally, the sources of all in-copyright material should be acknowledged. In some cases citing the creator and title of the reproduced work is regarded as sufficient information, but copyright holders will usually specify a fuller form of acknowledgement. The placing of the acknowledgement may also be specified, for instance immediately below the illustration or quotation. Where acknowledgements are not included in the text, a complete list in alphabetical order of copyright holders should be provided in the preliminary pages or at the end of the book.

Libel

Libel law is an extremely complex field but, very briefly, here are a few basic points for the publisher (and self-publisher) to bear in mind.

A libel is a defamatory statement in permanent form, for example in writing, whereas a slander is such a statement made in a temporary form like speech. A statement is defamatory if (a) it is untrue and (b) it damages a person's reputation. The person doesn't have to be mentioned by name: he or she only needs to be identifiable as the person intended. Nor need the defamatory statement be direct: it may be implied or in the form of an innuendo. While the dead cannot be

Can authors give permission to reproduce their work?

It's important to remember that if a work is currently in print the author will almost certainly have given the publisher the right to negotiate permissions. This means that a direct approach to the author is usually inappropriate, no matter how well you know him or her; you should approach the publisher. The same applies to illustrative work where it is held by, say, a museum – requests for permission to reproduce such work should be directed to the museum, not to the artist or photographer.

libelled, it is possible for living persons to be defamed by association. The fact that defamatory statements have been published previously is no defence.

If you as a publisher have the slightest doubt about a text, you should insist that the author identifies any potentially libellous statements and agrees to delete them. Even where an author asserts that a statement is true, most publishers are reluctant to spend time, money and emotional effort to have the truth of a statement tested in court (the burden of proof lies with the publisher). It is a fraught area and it is often wiser simply to delete or amend risky material. If you decide to seek legal advice, remember that it will almost certainly be expensive, and that the cost will have to be added to the budget.

Don't forget that if you publish a libel, albeit unintentionally, it could be financially and professionally ruinous, even if the author has agreed to indemnify you against costs – all copies of the offending book will have to be withdrawn from sale and/or destroyed, you may have to make (and pay for) a prominent public apology in the newspapers, and your credibility with the book trade and media will be permanently damaged.

Royalties

A royalty is an agreed percentage of the revenue made on the sale of a book, paid to the author at agreed intervals. Royalties are traditionally based on the retail price of the book, although recent changes in the book trade, especially the escalating buying power of the chains, has led some publishers to use net receipts as a base. For most small-scale publishing, however, the traditional method based on retail price remains the best approach. This can be modified by adjustments to protect the publisher when discount levels are high and to reward the author when sales levels are high.

For paperback books, the method of paying royalties might look something like this:

> On copies sold at a discount of up to 40 per cent – 7.5 per cent of retail price on sales up to 5,000 copies; 9 per cent of retail price on sales up to 10,000 copies and 10 per cent of retail price on sales above 10,000 copies;

> On copies sold at a discount of between 41 and 49 per cent – 5 per cent of retail price on sales up to 5,000 copies; 6.5 per

cent of retail price on sales up to 10,000 copies and 7.5 per cent of retail price on sales above 10,000 copies;

> On copies sold at a discount of 50 per cent and over – 3.75 per cent of retail price on sales up to 5,000 copies; 5.5 per cent of retail price on sales up to 10,000 copies and 6.5 per cent of retail price on sales above 10,000 copies.

Standard royalties on hardback books would generally follow a similar structure, but would begin at a top rate of 10 per cent of the retail price, with other rates adjusted roughly pro rata.

As explained earlier, it is not compulsory to pay an advance on royalties; where possible, try to persuade the author to wait until you both have a better idea of the book's sales performance. However, if you are paying an advance it should be calculated on the basis of no more than half of the estimated total royalties which would be payable if all the books were to sell out (remember to deduct free issue books from the quantity when you're doing the calculation).

Publisher/author agreements

Agreements between publishers and authors (or artists or photographers) can be fairly lengthy legal documents covering every foreseeable contingency in highly formal language – samples can be seen in books like *Clark's Publishing Agreements: A Book of Precedents* (see Bibiography). Many of the clauses will provide for eventualities that are unlikely to arise in the case of smaller local publishers, such as film rights, or merchandising rights for spin-off products like duvet covers or pencil cases, or perhaps the sale of translation rights to publishers in the Far East.

Provided both parties agree and care is taken to cover the main essential elements, a shorter, simpler agreement, formally signed and dated by both parties, is in many cases sufficient for the small publisher. These essential elements include:

- the names and addresses of both parties (author and publisher)
- the date of the agreement
- the title (or working title) of the proposed book (usually called 'the Work')
- a formal warranty from the author that he/she is the copyright holder of the Work and is legally entitled to enter into the present agreement
- formal warranties from the author that the Work contains nothing unlawful (for example, material which is libellous, obscene, improper, blasphemous or in breach of the Official Secrets Act), and a formal undertaking by the author that he/she will indemnify the publisher against all actions, proceedings, costs etc that arise out of any breach of the warranties given by the author
- a formal undertaking by the author that during the term of the agreement he/she will not prepare or publish a work which could be reasonably considered to compete with, or limit the sales of, the proposed Work
- (where the Work has not yet been delivered) an agreed date for the author to deliver the completed Work to the publisher's satisfaction
- the author's undertaking to license certain agreed rights to the publisher (for example, the right to publish the proposed book in the English language within a defined territory such as 'British & Commonwealth'), in return for certain payments

- an undertaking from the publisher to publish the book in a specified binding (hardback or paperback), within a specified price band and within a given time, unless prevented by circumstances beyond his/her control
- the amount and timing of the publisher's payments to the author (see panel on royalties, p.16)
- a provision for the termination of the contract under certain circumstances (for example, the reversion of rights to the author in the case of the book being out of print for a specified period of time)

Once you have agreed the main headings of the agreement with the author, you should ask an experienced solicitor to draw up a proposed agreement for consideration and (after any problems have been ironed out) signature by both parties – the legal fee will be money well spent.

Finally, don't feel that because you have a good relationship with the author that you don't need to draw up a formal agreement. Details of what was agreed orally can fade in the memory as time goes by, and the ups and downs of the publishing process can fray both nerves and tempers. For these reasons, it is essential for both parties to be able to refer to a written record of what was agreed at the outset and you should not under any circumstances proceed without a formal agreement. In addition, you should make a practice of always following up any sort of interchange at which decisions were made by sending the author a written note of the points agreed.

First steps

As a publisher, you will be presented with proposed books in all sorts of states, from a scribbled-in exercise book to a CD-Rom. Nowadays, a double-spaced word-processed electronic document is more or less essential for fast, effective editing, typesetting and design, so your first step is to make sure that one exists. (This applies whether you are self-publishing or publishing someone else's work.) Most publishers use Microsoft Word to ensure compatibility as the text passes from hand to hand during the editing process, with each stage being carefully saved, titled and dated.

Producing a word-processed script is usually regarded as the author's responsibility but occasionally you may have to arrange it yourself (if so, remember to cost it into your budget). In either case, you should check with the author (or yourself if you are the author) that this is the final version, as changes will become increasingly costly and time-consuming from now on. You will also need to print out a complete hard-copy (i.e. on paper) version of the final word-processed text (it's a good idea to date and archive any old hard copies at this stage to avoid confusion).

Now you're ready to begin the editing process.

> ' you will be presented with proposed books in all sorts of states, from a scribbled-in exercise book to a CD-Rom '

Can a computer replace an editor?

A word about modern technology and editing. In spite of its sophistication, computer software can never be a substitute for a careful copy-editor. It can carry out spell-checks (but what about unusual dialect or jargon words?), it can point out basic grammar mistakes (but what if your writer is deliberately bending the rules for effect?). What it certainly can't do is to spot contextual spelling mistakes (like 'their' instead of 'there' or 'they're'), errors of fact, misleading or inconsistent information, potential libel, inelegant phrasing, unintentional humour, ambiguity and many other common mistakes – somewhat comfortingly, we still need the human eye and brain for all of those.

Typescript The copy-editor should ensure that the entire copy-edited typescript is numbered in sequence so that there is no doubt in the typesetter's mind about the running order of the material. The numbers should be written in ringed pencil on the bottom right-hand corner of each page.
Print-ready copy The copy-editor's final preparation of the material to be presented to the printer should include a thorough check of the page numbers (also called 'folios'). The running order of the preliminary pages (i.e. every page that falls before page 1 of the main text) should be clearly indicated to the printer by the use of lower-case roman numerals (i, ii, iii, iv etc). Although every page has a number, these numbers will not be shown on every page of the prelims in the printed book. In particular, page numbers should *never* appear on the half-title, title, imprint, dedication or epigraph pages or on any blank pages.
Page numbering in standard arabic numerals (1, 2, 3, 4 etc) should begin on the first page of the main text, which should always be a right-hand page (recto). Page numbers should not be printed on blank pages or on pages containing illustrations or tables extending into the margin; such pages should however be counted in the pagination sequence.
As page numbers should make it easy for the reader to navigate the book, they are usually centred at the foot of the page, or towards the outer edge of the top or bottom. A design using less traditional positioning is also acceptable, always providing that the reader can find the numbers quickly.

Editing

The main aim of editing couldn't be simpler: it's to make sure that there are no obstacles between the writer's intention and the reader's understanding. The editor's job is to find and remove any such problems before the script goes for typesetting. Achieving this simple aim can actually be quite complex, requiring a variety of skills from a sound grasp of punctuation and grammar to the sensitive touch needed to negotiate editorial points with a nervously protective author. For this reason, you may wish to consider using the services of an experienced freelance editor.

Editing can be broken down into three main categories:

1 Substantive editing

In substantive editing, the editor considers the proposed book as a whole and works with the author to improve it. There are some important questions to ask at this stage. Is the material well organised and presented? Are there any unnecessary repetitions or irritating gaps in the information? What about the proposed length of the book and the level of the writing – are they appropriate for the target readership? Is there potentially libellous material or possible plagiarism? If there are illustrations, are they of good reproductive quality and do they and their captions complement and enhance the text? Will it be necessary to obtain (and possibly pay for) permission for the use of illustrations or for quoted material from other sources?

It is essential to involve the author closely at the substantive editing stage – after all, the book will be published under his or her name, not the editor's. Changes may be made either by the author working on the editor's suggested improvements, or by the editor with the agreement of the author. This is the stage at which diplomacy and understanding are vital, as some authors may be touchy about perceived criticism. From the very start of the relationship, it should be made clear that the editor is on the author's side, with the shared intention of making the proposed book as readable and fault-free as it can possibly be.

While these negotiations with the author can take place at a meeting or by letter or phone, nowadays they are usually carried out via email. Provided both parties are reasonably computer-literate this is the most efficient method.

2 Copy-editing

In copy-editing, the word-processed script is examined in close detail – sentence by sentence and word by word – for sense, accuracy and consistency. Keeping always in mind the basic aim of removing any obstacles between the writer's intention and the reader's understanding, the copy-editor assesses and if necessary corrects punctuation, grammar, word order, spelling, hyphenation etc. Care should also be taken in checking that any data presented in table form agree with the text and that captions agree with picture content. It's also important to check that any note numbers in the text are numbered consecutively and correspond to their footnotes or endnotes.

Some aspects of the copy-editing process can be quite straightforward – for example, it could be changing something like 'she poured over the book' to 'she pored over the book' (thereby removing unintentional humour as well as incorrect spelling), or 'he jumped onto the horse wearing his spurs' to 'wearing his spurs, he jumped onto the horse' (this time, it's rearranging the word order that has got rid of the unintentional humour). It's also relatively simple to ensure consistency throughout the text in, say, the spelling of a name or the use of single and/or double quotation marks (this is now even easier with a computer 'find and replace' facility). It's also important to check for consistency – in a novel, does a character's name or physical description change without explanation halfway through? (This is usually a hangover from an earlier draft.) Or does a place name like 'Ballymacarett' suddenly become 'Ballymacarrett'? (Placenames with Irish origins are particularly prone to this kind of shifting about.)

> ' make sure that there are no obstacles between the writer's intention and the reader's understanding '

Other matters are harder to resolve, and even the most knowledgeable editors have to refer to dictionaries, encyclopaedias, internet search engines like Google and specialist manuals like *Butcher's Copy-editing* (see Bibliography). Without such props, common sense can be an unreliable guide – for instance would you have known without looking it up that current usage has 'jobcentre' as one word, 'job lot' as two words and 'job-share' as a hyphenated word? Or whether it's correct to say 'she ran 9 miles' or 'she ran nine miles'? Or whether you should use roman type

Footnotes and endnotes

With the exception of some academic or specialist publications, most modern books do not use footnotes or endnotes. Where possible, information is incorporated into the text rather than presented separately, for example 'the *Ballywhatsit News* of 18 June 1887 reported that "tension was high in the town"' is preferred to 'a local newspaper reported that "tension was high in the town"', with a superscript number referring the reader to a footnote (at the bottom of the page) or an endnote (at the end of the book or the chapter) giving the details about the newspaper source.

If a note reference system is unavoidable, modern practice is to use endnotes rather than footnotes, with superscript numbers referring to a 'Notes' section, which is arranged by chapter and (ideally) page number and presented at the end of the book.

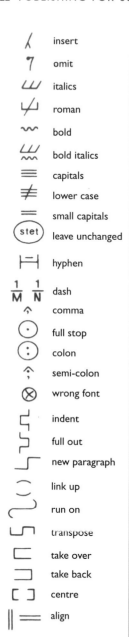

⅄	insert
7	omit
⊔⊔	italics
⊬	roman
∿	bold
⊔⊔	bold italics
≡	capitals
≢	lower case
=	small capitals
(stet)	leave unchanged
⊢⊣	hyphen
¹⁄M ¹⁄N	dash
↑	comma
⊙	full stop
⊙	colon
⌃	semi-colon
⊗	wrong font
	indent
	full out
	new paragraph
	link up
	run on
	transpose
	take over
	take back
[ ]	centre
‖ =	align

(i.e. ordinary type like this) or italic type (*like this*) for poem titles or ships' names?

Most copy-editors find it effective to read through the hard copy first, marking any obvious errors in pencil before going on to the on-screen copy-edit of the word-processed document. As the work proceeds, the copy-editor should be compiling a style sheet – a simple hand-ruled grid of twenty-four boxes, one for each letter of the alphabet except **x**, **y** and **z**, which squeeze together into the last box. Using the boxes to list each relevant word alphabetically, the copy-editor should indicate the style adopted for unusual words or names, or the preference where a word has more than one acceptable spelling (e.g. realise/realize). She/he should also show whether certain words should be capitalised (e.g. army/Army) or hyphenated etc. This sheet will ensure consistency of style throughout the text and become a useful point of reference at subsequent proofreading stages.

Any suggested rewriting, changes in word order or to factual information (where the editor has discovered an incorrect date, for instance) are then highlighted in colour in the on-screen version, if necessary with an explanatory note (also in colour) in square brackets. Smaller changes such as corrections of obvious spelling or punctuation mistakes usually do not need to be highlighted.

The copy-edited script is then sent to the author in its entirety as an attachment via email, with a request for on-screen responses (using a different colour) to the proposed changes. In an ideal world, the author will agree to all the changes right away. More realistically, negotiations will continue by email until both author and editor are happy. The copy-editor should keep and maintain a master document that includes all agreed changes. (If preferred, all of this liaison process can be carried out face to face at meetings or by phone or letter.)

Before the finalised copy-edited script goes to the typesetter, ask the author to read it through very carefully one more time; as subsequent changes will cause delay and expense you should impress on him/her that this is the last chance to make any. (This advice applies equally in the case of self-publishers.) Given the fallibility of memory, it's prudent to keep a written record of the author's responses and of shared decisions about changes and rewritings.

3 Preparing material for presentation to the typesetter

The copy-editor, having agreed all necessary changes with the author, now makes a final check that all the material is complete and in perfect order before it is passed to the typesetter.

All the parts of the proposed book should be clearly identified, as should different grades of headings and subheadings and pieces of text (e.g. long quotations) requiring different indents and/or point sizes. The positioning of illustrations, captions, maps, tables and diagrams should be clearly marked. Prelims (preliminary pages like half-title, title, imprint, contents, dedication, acknowledgements etc) and any end matter (bibliography, index etc) should also be included.

The typesetter (who nowadays is sometimes also the designer) will need the finalised copy-edited text in the form of an email attachment (usually a Word document) or a disk, as well as a hard copy. Where typesetting is being done separately, the material should first be passed to the designer to add technical instructions for the typesetter.

> Faced with the material in paged form, some authors may be tempted to make changes to the text.

Proofing

First proof

Once the text has been typeset into page form, it needs to be checked, or 'proofed', to make sure that no new errors have crept in during typesetting.

One of the many efficiencies of working with a word-processed script is that the typesetter does not have to key in all the words again, thus minimising the level of error. However, problems can arise with layout, pagination, line breaks, hyphenation, position of illustrations, captions, tables etc and these must all be carefully checked. It is good practice for the proofreader to be someone other than the copy-editor, as one's own mistakes are often the hardest to spot. This is especially true if you are self-publishing.

Simultaneously, the author should also be given a set of the first proofs and asked to mark any errors. Faced with the material in paged form, some authors may be tempted to make changes to the text. As this will introduce extra cost (and after all, the author has already been warned

Proofreading marks

You will find it time well spent to obtain a list of standard proofreading marks and get yourself accustomed to using them – properly applied, they are by far the most efficient method. It is in theory possible to indicate corrections, additions, deletions etc without using such marks, but because this method carries a higher risk of confusion it is not generally recommended. A list of proofreading marks, like those opposite, can be found in *New Hart's Rules* (see Bibliography) or you can download an Acrobat PDF version from www.ideography.co.uk/proof/marks.html.

that the copy-edit stage is the last chance for changes), the temptation should be resisted, except where, for example, errors of fact have been spotted.

The author's marked-up set of proofs is then collated with the proofreader's set to create a master set which is returned to the typesetter for correction.

Second and subsequent proofs

Except in exceptional circumstances, the author's last sight of the script is at first-proof stage; from now on, corrections (and sometimes corrections to corrections) will be handled by the publisher's proofreaders, who will mark up each set of proofs and if necessary return it to the typesetter for further corrections. At the end of the proofing process, even if you are satisfied that all is correct and in good order, it is essential to have one last final read.

How to read proofs effectively

Most of us read a book or newspaper quickly to grasp the sense of what the writer is trying to say, mostly disregarding small mistakes in spelling, punctuation or grammar. A proofreader on the other hand needs to read slowly and carefully, looking out for errors that a faster reading will miss. These can include anything from spelling mistakes and grammatical howlers to brackets that open and never close (although strictly speaking all of these should have been corrected at the earlier copy-editing stage).

It is much more difficult for the inexperienced proofreader to spot typographical errors, including:

- gappy or squeezed lines (where spaces between words are too wide or too narrow)
- inconsistent leading (i.e. unequal depths between lines)
- inconsistent use of typefaces or point sizes
- folios (i.e. page numbers) that are inconsistent in position or style (you should also check that folios run consecutively, with no repeats or breaks)
- inconsistent indentations
- inconsistent headings, including chapter headings, subheadings and running heads
- line breaks with misleading hyphenation (eg leg-end, the-rapist, read-just)

most of us red a book or newspaper Quickly
to grasp the sense of what the writer trying to is
say, mostly disregarding small mistakes in
spelling, punctuation or grammer.

A proofreader on the hand other need to read
slowly and carefully, looking out for errors
than a faster reading miss.

Final read

It's always a good idea for the final read to be done, if possible, by someone with a fresh eye, i.e. not the copy-editor or the proofreader. Remember that this exercise is purely to pick up typographical mistakes or any remaining errors of fact (although in theory there shouldn't be any at this stage). It is *not* the time to suggest major changes to structure or approach.

As well as checking the main text, illustrations, captions etc, the final reader should also make sure that all other material is present and correct, i.e. prelims (half-title, title, imprint and contents pages etc) and any end matter (bibliography, index etc).

All being well, the material is now ready for the designer to prepare it for printing.

> ' It's always a good idea for the final read to be done, if possible, by someone with a fresh eye. '

ISBN 978-0-9557419-0-6

9 780955 741906

ISBNs and bar codes

An ISBN (International Standard Book Number) is a unique 13-digit identification number assigned to a publication; it should be displayed on the reverse of the title page and on the outside back cover. It is used by booksellers, libraries and publishers for ordering, listing and stock control. There is no legal requirement for an ISBN and it conveys no form of legal or copyright protection. If however the publication is to be sold through retail outlets or Internet bookstores, it is essential.

The UK International Standard Book Numbering Agency allocates the numbers; there is a charge for this service and the numbers themselves can only be purchased in blocks of at least ten numbers. Hardback and paperback editions of the same book will have different ISBNs and a new number is also needed for new or revised editions. It takes up to ten working days for the agency to issue the numbers but ideally an ISBN should be applied for as soon as the book's title is decided upon.

The bar code for a book corresponds to its ISBN and should be displayed on the outside back cover. Like the ISBN, it is essential if the book is to be sold through retail outlets or Internet stores. Most printers will generate a bar code from the ISBN for a small fee, or you can order one yourself from a specialist company such as Axicon.

For more information contact:

ISBNs UK ISBN Agency
Nielson Bookdata
3rd Floor, Midas House
Goldsworth Road
Woking
Surrey, GU21 6LQ.
PHONE: 0870 777 8710
email: isbn@nielsenbookdata.co.uk
web: www.isbn.nielsonbookdata.co.uk

Bar codes Axicon Auto ID Ltd
Church Road
Weston on the Green
Oxford
OX25 3QP
PHONE: 01869 351 166
web: www.axicon.com/barcoding.htm

35
35
35
35
31
30
32
32
31
31
30

Design

The look of a book is a crucial part of its success and many otherwise interesting publications fail because of ineffective design. An attractive cover will entice bookshop browsers to stop and glance through a book – the first step to a purchase. But there is much more to book design than attractive covers, and a working knowledge of basic book design principles will be a great help to you as a publisher. This applies whether you are using a professional book designer or attempting to design the book yourself.

Using a professional book designer

This may seem an expensive option if you are on a tight budget, but it could save you money in the end. It will certainly save you a lot of time and frustration. Apart from having the tricks of the trade at their fingertips, professional designers will often do the typesetting and liaise with the printer on your behalf. Their early advice will help you to arrive at an economic specification for your book which will allow keener printers' estimates, and by troubleshooting and keeping an eye on quality during printing, they will free you up to concentrate on advance publicity and marketing.

It's important to develop a good working relationship with your designer, especially when it comes to the briefing (where you explain the ideas you have for how the book might look) and to the presentation of ideas and roughs for your approval. Be clear about your requirements but not inflexible – keep your mind open to new ideas and advice based on experience.

Designing the book yourself

The first thing to remember is that the design should communicate the essence of the book by reflecting its content in a clear and stimulating way. Above all, don't over-design it with an excessive mixture of typefaces and layouts – in almost all books, design should be a quiet but effective medium of the message, not an all-singing, all-dancing performer. The typographical options offered by desktop publishing packages are tempting, but use them sparingly.

One of the most useful things you can do is to spend time in bookshops and libraries looking critically at the elements of book design

– covers, bindings, paper quality, formats, layouts, typefaces and point sizes, position of illustrations and captions etc – and making notes of what attracts you and what doesn't.

Elements of good book design

FORMAT The first thing to decide on is the format of the book – that is, its shape (portrait, landscape or square) and its size (that is, its height and width in millimetres). There are a number of factors to be considered here: economic use of paper (take your printer's advice on this, as there's no point choosing an unusual size if you finish up paying for binfuls of wasted paper – do avoid A4 and A5 sizes, though, as they look unattractive in a book); appropriateness to content (it would be odd for a novel to have a landscape format, for instance, while it might suit a photographic book very well); plenty of design scope for effective, uncrowded layouts of text and illustrations; and even whether your book will fit bookshop and library shelves.

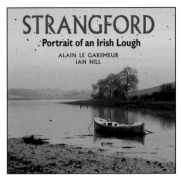

280 x 250 mm

245 x 170 mm

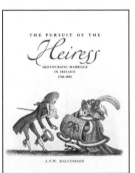

265 x 196 mm

216 x 135 mm

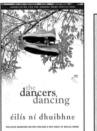

198 x 129 mm

186 x 122 mm

GRID AND LAYOUT While good cover design is an important marketing tool, the author's message will be carried in the body of the book. For this reason, the interior design should have visual coherence and consistency that create a clean, uncluttered look and allow the reader to concentrate on the content. A considerable amount of thought should therefore be given to the grid system and layout of the pages and openings.

A grid system is basically a set of decisions about such things as margin widths (on the left, right, top and bottom of the page); the proportions of the area taken up by text and images; the position of headings, page numbers, and so on. It can be very simple, as with a novel, or quite

Frontispiece and title page   Chapter opening

complex, as with an illustrated children's book.

Along with the grid system, a well thought-out layout plan will streamline decisions about the shape and position of illustrations in relation to the text, or what a chapter or section opening should look like, or how preliminary matter such as title and imprint pages should be handled. It needn't be a straitjacket; a good one will offer a variety of choices, allowing the creation of uncluttered openings that still look flexible and lively.

TYPOGRAPHY   As with other elements of design, typography (i.e. typeface, point size, line width, leading, alignment etc) should be regarded as a medium for conveying the author's meaning – if it is gimmicky or lacking in coherence it will have failed in its purpose.

When choosing a typeface for your book, stick to one family of type, for example Garamond, Sabon or Bembo. You will find that this offers you plenty of choice while maintaining the overall coherence that marks a well-designed book. For the main text, a serif face is preferable to a sans serif one, which is usually reserved for display or captions.

For ease of reading, most modern books use a point size of 10 or 11 with a leading (i.e. the space between lines of text) of 12 or 13. Similarly,

an optimum line width of 12 words (or 65 characters) is considered the most comfortable – if it is longer, the eye has too far to travel to pick up the text at the beginning of the next line.

Having made these decisions about the type, your next one will be about its arrangement on the page, its alignment. The main text in a book is usually fully justified, that is with both left and right sides aligned in straight lines. This can be varied in the case of captions, displayed material etc, where the text can be justified to the right only (this is known as ragged left), to the left only (ragged right), or centred.

If you are doing the typesetting yourself, bear in mind that

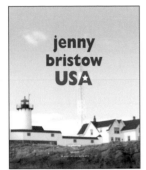

Title page

modern style has only one space between sentences, that there is usually no paragraph indent at the beginning of chapters or sections and that quoted material from other sources should be displayed to differentiate it from the main text (usually by a smaller point size and wider indentation).

Remember that, while they may seem time-consuming, these simple typesetting conventions will make a tremendous difference to the appearance and readability of your book.

PAPER The appropriate choice of paper can make all the difference to the appearance of a book. Don't use a pure white paper, as it is hard on the eyes, and make sure to choose one that is opaque enough to stop print on the reverse side from showing through. Avoid papers that are overly light or heavy in weight (to give you a basis for comparison, this book is printed on a paper with a weight of 100 gsm). Papers with a shiny rather than a matt finish are generally unsuitable for text-based books – they look old-fashioned, they're too reflective and, because they are usually heavier, they can increase postage and distribution costs. On the other hand, a good quality glossy paper can enhance the appearance of an illustrated book.

Most book printers stock a limited range of papers and by and large you should be able to find something to suit you – when you're deciding which printer to use, ask to see samples of the papers and of what they look like when they're printed and bound. Remember that choosing a non-stock paper can both increase the bill and delay production while the printer arranges a special order with the paper manufacturer.

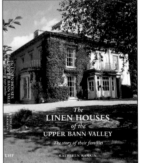

THE COVER To most people, book design means cover design. As we have seen, there is a lot more to it than that, but there is no doubt that when it comes to sales the cover design can make or break a book. Jostling for attention with all the other covers in the bookshop, it has to attract customers and make them want to stop for a closer look. Long before the book reaches the shop, the cover will have been instrumental in persuading the bookseller to place an order. It will also need to make an impact in any ads, flyers, posters, catalogues or websites.

As well as being a crucial marketing tool, the cover has to carry a lot of information on its front, back and spine (plus on its front and back flaps in some cases).

FRONT COVER The most important elements of the front cover are the image and the title and author's name. They all need to evoke the content of the book as well as attracting buyers – not as simple as it might seem.

back flap | spine | front flap

author's biographical note

blurb

publisher's address and cover credit details

ISBN and price

bar code | publisher's name/logo | Title and author's name

IMAGE   The cover image may be an illustration (e.g. a painting or drawing) or a photograph, specially commissioned or already in existence. While it should give an impression of the contents, it isn't always necessary for it to be a direct reflection. If you are publishing a history of a school, for instance, it might make a more arresting cover if you used a dynamic image of children in a classroom rather than a static photograph of the façade.

You may know of a painting or photograph you think would be perfect, either in its entirety or cropped. As with all art works, it's essential that you trace the copyright holders of such images and negotiate permission to reproduce them. It's also vital to obtain a first-class reproduction of the image – without it, the printed cover will be of disappointingly poor quality. On no account try to use a photocopy from another book or a newspaper, or a downloaded image from the web. It may look great on your screen but will almost certainly reproduce disappointingly.

On the other hand, you may decide to commission a new illustration or photograph for your cover. Once you've found an artist or photographer whose style you like and who is willing to take on the commission, make sure that both of you are on the same wavelength about the nature of the job, the financial arrangements and the schedule. Even if you know the person well, it's a good idea to prepare a simple letter of agreement for signature by both parties. At the first briefing you should explain your concept for the book, its target readership and its dimensions. Based on this, plus a copy of the text and some indication from you on where you want the title and author's name to be placed, the artist or photographer should prepare a few roughs of the cover for you. Your chosen rough will then be worked up into a final image that hopefully both of you will be pleased with.

Finally, it's worth remembering that it's not compulsory to have a cover

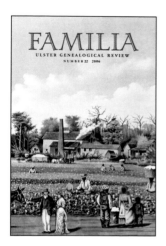

image as such – a purely graphic design, with strong typography and confident use of colour and contrast can be extremely effective for certain types of books.

TITLE DESIGN Once you've chosen a cover image, experiment with superimposing the title, subtitle (if any) and author's name on it. Increasingly with paperbacks, the front cover also displays a short line of promotional text or an endorsement from a celebrity, so include that too if you're using it.

Try a variety of typefaces and styles to find ones that will make an impact by being easy to read and avoiding fussiness and clutter. Use as large a type size as you can for the title and a smaller one for the author's name. (Except in the case of a very famous author, having the author's name larger than the title usually reflects an inflated ego – it's the book's contents you're trying to sell, after all.)

Choose a colour scheme that enhances the image and helps to create the overall impression you want. Imagine your book displayed with hundreds of others in a shop or library – will it stand out, making people want to investigate further? Be as fresh and original as you can – it might be tempting to imitate the style of a current bestseller, but you're likely to find your book lost in a horde of other copy-cats.

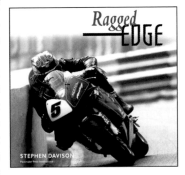

SPINE Traditionally, a book spine simply displays title, subtitle if any, author's name and publisher's logo, arranged to read from the top to the bottom. However, because today's crowded bookshops mean that most books cannot be displayed face-out, the spine may be the only chance the book has to shout its wares. For that reason, many spines now include a small illustration, usually lifted from the cover image.

BACK COVER With a paperback book, the back cover has to work hard to carry the sort of information that is usually carried in the front and back flaps of a hardback – a blurb describing the book, perhaps a photo and short biography of the author, advance praise for the book or previous critical acclaim for the author, the price, the bar code, a design credit for the cover, a permission line for the cover image and the publisher's logo.

Some of these elements are essential (the bar code and price, for example), but it's obvious that some decisions are going to have to be made about the others – it's all but impossible to include all this material and still have an effective back cover design that will attract buyers. Look critically at each element with the marketing in mind. Does the blurb need to be that long? Is using the author's photo another example of ego-boosting? Could his/her biography be moved to inside the book, perhaps taking the place of the half-title on the first page?

Having boiled the text down to manageable proportions, the same principles of design – a lively, harmonious blend of typography, colour and contrast – apply here as with the front cover.

With a hardback book, the back cover can be blank (using a solid colour or tint that tones with the front and spine), or display a reduced version of the cover image, or give some information about the book, especially advance praise.

FRONT AND BACK FLAPS Part of the cover (strictly speaking 'dust jacket') for a hardback (or for a paperback with 'French flaps'), front and back flaps are usually very simply designed, without the razzamatazz of the exterior. The front flap will usually carry the blurb and price, with the back flap displaying a photograph and short biography of the author, credits for the cover designer and author's photographer, a permission line for the cover image, and the publisher's name and address.

Back cover of
Early Belfast

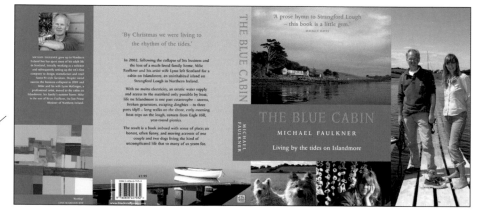

Back flap with author photograph and biography

The Blue Cabin is a paperback book with 'French flaps' and the inside cover used as endpapers – see opposite

BINDING For a hardback, you will have decisions to make about the type and colour of the binding cloth or paper. Liaise with your printer on these – again, he will be able to direct you about the most economical use of material (he may not have your preferred colour in stock, for instance, but be able to show you a stock colour that is an acceptable substitute, as well as being cheaper).

ENDPAPERS When you open a hardback book, the sheet pasted to the back of the front cover together with the page facing it (the flyleaf) are

known as the endpapers – the same arrangement applies at the back of the book. Don't overlook the design potential of these – by choosing a solid colour that matches or tones with the dust jacket and binding boards you will enhance the overall look of the book, or by using them to display, say, a map of the book's locale you will add greatly to the reader's enjoyment.

Printed endpapers for Strangford: Portrait of an Irish Lough

INSIDE COVERS Publishers are increasingly using the inside covers of paperbacks, especially at the back, to carry extra promotional material, for example information (including cover reproductions) about other books in the same series, or by the same author. This is effective and doesn't cost much more than leaving the inside covers blank.

Typesetting

While it is possible to typeset your book yourself using a desktop publishing software package, it is very difficult to achieve a professional appearance overall and to meet the printer's requirements at handover time. For this reason I would strongly recommend that you use a professional typesetter – your printer should be able to recommend

Inside cover of The Blue Cabin

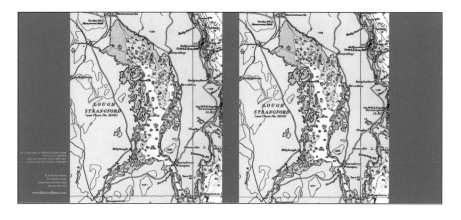

someone. Alternatively, as mentioned earlier, if you are using a professional designer you may find that he or she will offer typesetting as part of the package.

Printing and binding

You will have chosen your printer at an earlier stage when you were preparing your budget, based on book-printing experience and written estimates of price and schedule etc. Keep in touch regarding schedule, particularly if it looks as though you may not be able to meet the deadline for handing over the print-ready material. Don't assume that missing the handover deadline by, say, ten days means that the book will be delayed by ten days – you may have lost your place in the queue of orders and have to wait longer before your job can be slotted in again. On the other hand, some other customers might also be late, allowing things to be speeded through for you. The important thing is always to communicate with the printer about any anticipated delays.

Visiting the printing floor while your book is going through is an exciting experience and, provided you have made an appointment and don't get in the way too much, most printers will be happy to show off their printing equipment and expertise. Their awareness that you will be looking at the quality of your book as it is being printed may even enhance their quality control. With their consent, you could also make this into a photo-opportunity, with your author examining the first sheets coming off the press. In any case you should ask to see printer's proofs, especially with illustrated books.

Discuss your delivery preferences with the printer, for example exact delivery address and convenient time etc. Remember they will be used to fork-lifting pallets full of books into large warehouses. If it would suit you better to have the books packed in robust cardboard boxes, clearly marked with the quantities of copies in each, that's what you should request.

Glued or sewn?

You will also have to decide whether the pages are going to be glued or sewn. Sewn is a more expensive but sensible option for books that will get heavy wear, like reference or cookery books, but otherwise modern gluing methods are usually more than adequate.

Publicity and promotion

Traditionally, publicising a book requires a two-pronged approach. Obviously, you want as many potential buyers as possible to know about your book, but you also need to make sure that the actual buying of copies is simple and hassle-free. This means that your publicity campaign should have two main target areas: (1) the print and broadcast media, to raise awareness of your book and (2) booksellers, library suppliers and appropriate retailers, to ensure that copies are in stock when customers look for them.

The 'Sales and distribution' section will cover the second group, as well as giving some advice about direct and/or online selling. However, it's vital to maintain an integrated, coherent approach to both targets – it's pointless having brilliant publicity if the book isn't easily available, and almost as pointless having piles of your book in the shops if nobody has heard of it.

Working with the media

Always remember that you're facing enormous competition for media space – newspapers, magazines, radio and television programmes are swamped with promotional campaigns for all sorts of products, including books. It's therefore essential that your publicity is distinctive, timely and properly targeted.

Try to put yourself in the journalists' shoes – why would they want to give precious space or airtime to *your* book when there are scores of other products clamouring for attention? Try to find ways of convincing them that there's something special about it that will genuinely interest their readers, listeners or viewers. Look for angles, perhaps attaching a handwritten note to your promotional material pointing out, for example, that the author was born/educated/lives/works in the journalist's catchment area, or reminding him or her that the book coincides with an important event or anniversary.

Make sure you're in touch with the right person – don't rely on old information or on blindly sending material to 'the editor', 'the producer' etc. Phone newspaper offices and broadcasting stations and find out who's currently responsible for book reviews and features, or for your book's subject area. While you should get across your enthusiasm for the book, don't go over the top about it and don't on any account harass the journalist or get aggressive – it's counter-productive and could queer your pitch for other projects (or indeed with other journalists – word soon gets around about over-pushy publishers and authors).

Advance publicity

It's often useful to send advance information in the form of a personal letter to the appropriate journalists, enclosing an attractive advance information sheet (see sample, p.40) and a printed cover if you have one – say, four or five weeks before publication for the print and radio media and longer for television. Follow this up after a few days with a friendly phone call (keep it brief!) explaining what's special about your book and offering author interviews, supply of photographs etc. By giving them plenty of time to prepare, you may get a lengthier feature or author profile when the book is published. And don't forget to invite them (and their photographers) to the launch if you're having one!

Review copies

Ideally the main publicity for a book should coincide with its first availability in the shops. Review copies should therefore be sent to the media around three weeks before publication date to allow time for reviewers to read the book and write the review. While production slippages often make this schedule unrealistic, resulting in reviews and other notices appearing some time after publication, it is nevertheless an effective target to keep in mind.

The review copy should be sent with a short press release giving details of author, title, price, publication date, blurb, information about the author and any advance praise (preview quotes) from notable people. Again, it's a good idea to send a personal letter or attach a note, addressing the journalist by name and reminding him or her of your earlier conversation. Use a padded envelope to post the book or, even better, to deliver it by hand, as it protects the book and looks more professional.

For the print media, you could include photographs of the author and/or images from the book, but make sure these are eye-catching and of good reproducible quality. Photographs aren't essential but will often be seized on by journalists trying to fill a page – and the old cliché about a picture telling a thousand stories means that any coverage of your book will attract more attention.

Don't waste time and money sending review copies to the large London or Dublin newspapers and magazines, unless you have a famous author or your subject is newsworthy on a national level. Instead, concentrate your efforts on your local media and, if appropriate, on specialist

Broadcast interviews

If you're lucky enough to land a radio or television interview, it's worth taking a bit of time to work out two or three main points about the book you want to get across and to go over them with the author (or yourself if you're the interviewee). Remember that you'll almost certainly have no more than a couple of minutes of airtime and that the presenter may have only skimmed the book or even the blurb. There's no point feeling disappointed or cross about this – it's a very pressurised business. In fact, lack of preparation on the presenter's part can often be turned to your advantage – he or she may even be relieved if you take the initiative and introduce quirky or interesting aspects of the book yourself.

magazines and websites further afield. In any case, keep a tight grip on the number of review copies you send out – you have to cast your bread on the waters to some extent, but remember that every book given away is one less to sell.

Launch parties

While many books are launched at a party on or around publication date, this is by no means compulsory – believe it or not, publishers sometimes throw launch parties just to please the author, without any real hope of generating extra publicity or sales. However, for the right sort of book there's no doubt that a well-planned event can create an extra buzz that will make a big difference to a book's success. It's also an opportunity to thank publicly the people who have helped in its production and can generate a great deal of goodwill simply by bringing the community together for the occasion.

There's no need to spend a lot of money on venue and catering – many successful launches take place in bookshops, with the publisher supplying wine and/or soft drinks and the

Signing sessions

Be careful with signing sessions in bookshops or other outlets. While celebrities can attract huge crowds to their signings, lesser-known authors can find the experience rather humiliating. There's nothing worse than a solitary author sitting behind a pile of unsold books for an hour or more, with everyone except relatives and friends (who will probably have acquired the book by then anyway) averting their eyes from his or her predicament.

Advertising

In most cases, it's more cost-effective to generate 'free' publicity in the form of reviews, features, author interviews, extracts etc and it's also generally felt that such publicity is more trusted by the public than advertisements. However, a few carefully placed advertisements in your local newspaper or an appropriate specialist magazine or website can be effective, needn't break the bank and may encourage journalists to give you more space in the editorial pages (but don't let yourself be pressurised into buying expensive advertising).

bookseller handling sales. With a non-trade venue like a church or community hall you can usually sell books directly to the guests, thereby saving the discount you would have had to give to a bookseller. In this case, bear in mind that you'll need help to run the sales point (remember to organise plenty of change) and the refreshments table – you need to be free to welcome and mingle with the guests and generally keep an eye on the smooth running of everything, including helping the press to round up people for photographs.

Invite plenty of people – more than the venue can accommodate as you're very unlikely to get anything like a 100-per-cent take-up. Include all the journalists you've been in touch with and notify newspaper photo-desks and broadcasting stations of the event, including the names of any notable people who will be attending. A well-known guest speaker will swell the crowd as well as adding prestige. Ideally, invitations should be sent out two or three weeks in advance and it's a good idea to enclose an informative flyer that includes a simple order form for the book; people who can't attend will often be glad of the opportunity to buy a copy.

Make sure there are some chairs for those who need them and keep the hospitality flowing – have the refreshments table near the entrance and send people round every so often to top up glasses or cups or to offer nibbles.

Keep speeches short and entertaining – you'll soon lose the goodwill of your guests if they have to stand through four or five lengthy addresses. Make it easy for them to buy the book and get it signed – have the sales point in a prominent position, with a small table for the author to sit at while signing, and be ready to rescue him or her tactfully if someone is holding up the queue. Guard against people assuming that the book is free by having copies only at the sales point, with the price prominently displayed – if you are not having the launch in a bookshop and are therefore not having to give away any trade discount at the event, you can increase sales by offering a special discount for the occasion.

Extra publicity

Don't rest on your laurels once the book has been launched – you can keep sales rolling by arranging readings, talks and exhibitions in libraries, schools, clubs, church halls etc. Make sure the book is available at all such events – authors are often happy to handle sales themselves if you give them a discount on the retail price.

Keep in touch with your media contacts – thank them for their coverage and tell them about anything interesting that happens around or after publication, for instance if there's a rush of buying that necessitates a speedy reprint or if the book is nominated for a prize.

Sales

It may sound obvious, but don't wait until the book is at the printers – or even being delivered – before you begin to work on sales. Remember that the best media publicity in the world is going to be wasted if your target customers can't easily find copies of the book to buy. It's vital that bookshops and other outlets learn about the book in sufficient time to place their orders and have copies on display by publication day. This means a lot of forward planning and determined footwork by you.

Advance sales material

Put together a set of advance information packs that are as attractive and user-friendly as you can make them. This doesn't have to be expensive – good ideas and eye-catching presentation are more important than costly printing and trendy folders. Each pack should be headed by a smart-looking one-page advance information sheet giving details of the book (author, title, format, price, ISBN and publication date) and of the publisher (publishing name, address, phone numbers, email address), along with a short well-written blurb, some information about the author and a few 'selling points' like local interest, anniversary tie-in, hoped-for media coverage etc. If you have exciting publicity and/or advertising plans, or 'promises' about media coverage, create another sheet showing these as bullet points. If you can arrange advance copies of the printed cover, or sample openings in the case of an illustrated book, include them in the pack.

The hunt for orders

Before you start contacting potential customers, decide on your trading terms – discount levels, length of credit, returns policy for unsold books etc (see 'Trading terms' below). Give yourself some flexibility to negotiate within discount bands that make financial sense to you but be determined not to give away more than you can afford. (This may sound obvious, but it's easy to get carried away when a buyer is waving a big order under your nose!)

ADVANCE INFORMATION

PUBLISHING FOR SUCCESS
A practical guide

ANNE TANNAHILL

'At its best, publishing is one of the most absorbing, challenging and rewarding pursuits imaginable.

At its worst, it is frustrating, exhausting and financially hazardous.

But what does a publisher actually do?'

paperback
80 pages
full colour throughout
illlustrated
ISBN 978-0-9557419-0-6
publication: March 2008
free on request

Published in response to demand from local publishers, this short guide provides a clear outline of the publishing process, with friendly, practical advice about sensible paths to follow and common pitfalls to avoid. Written by an experienced publisher, it is packed with helpful tips on financial management; legal aspects such as copyright and libel; editing, proofing, design, typesetting and printing; and publicity, sales and distribution. Also included is a list of funding sources and a directory of useful addresses, as well as a bibliography, a glossary of publishing terms and an index.

For further information please contact Monica McErlane at NIPR

Northern Ireland Publications Resource (NIPR) is an initiative sponsored by the Library & Information Services Council (Northern Ireland) with funding from the Department of Culture, Arts & Leisure (DCAL). It aims to acquire and preserve every book, pamphlet, periodical and report published in Northern Ireland since January 2000, and to create an accompanying bibliography. Thanks to the generosity of local publishers, NIPR is building an archive of Northern Ireland's unique publishing heritage.

Northern Ireland Publications Resource

Linen Hall Library,
17 Donegall Square North, Belfast BT1 5GB,
tel: +44 (0) 28 9032 1707, fax: +44 (0) 28 9043 8586,
email: **info@nibooks.org**

Belfast Central Library,
Royal Avenue, Belfast BT1 1EA, tel: +44 (0) 28 9024 2740,
fax: +44 (0) 28 9033 2819, email: **info@nibooks.org**

This guide has been generously sponsored by its printer, **W & G Baird Ltd of Antrim,** wgbaird@wgbaird.com, and was also financially supported by Awards for All, www.awardsforall.org.uk/ northernireland.

Two to three weeks before publication date, make personal visits to outlets you think might be persuaded to order the book – bookshops, newsagents, village shops, post offices, pubs, hotels etc. Ask to speak to the manager or buyer – if it turns out to be an inconvenient time, ask for an appointment at a time that suits them. (This is better than making a 'cold' phone call asking for an appointment because if your request is refused – as it almost certainly will be by larger shops – it leaves you stymied.)

When you find yourself face to face with a buyer, explain succinctly what's special about your book and why it will be worth their while to stock it. You may get an order at this point – if not, leave the advance information pack with him or her, making sure your contact details are prominently displayed. Call back in person once you have the finished book in your hand and speak to the buyer. Talk the book up again, emphasising any fresh news, further media promises etc. Offer to provide 'point-of-sale' material – small posters, flyers, bookmarks etc that will draw attention to the book and help the bookseller to sell more.

Finally, and most importantly, don't forget to close the sale by getting an actual order! Ask for an order number and enquire about invoicing requirements and delivery details (some shops may have a back-up store at another address, for instance, or there may be strict rules about times

Selling to Eason

Eason is a powerful presence in Irish bookselling by virtue of their huge wholesaling operation plus their twenty-five bookshops in Northern Ireland and thirty-six in the Republic. The headquarters are in Dublin and commercial publishers deal with Eason buyers there through a centralised ordering system.

However, because Eason is conscious of its responsibility to the community, they offer a simpler method for new and small publishers in Northern Ireland. With this method, the publisher currently sends an email to Robin Gourley at the Dublin headquarters, giving him information about the forthcoming book (rgourley@easonwholesale.com). This should include a short one-paragraph outline of the book, plus the following details: title, author, price, ISBN, publication date, contact name, phone number and email address. (If available, a copy of the cover and advance information sheet should also be sent.)

If Robin Gourley considers the book to be suitable he will write to the managers of the twenty-five NI bookshops giving them permission to stock the book if they wish to. The current stipulated discount level is 40 per cent off the retail price on a strictly sale-or-return basis, i.e. books will not be paid for until they have been sold. In practice, this means that ordered books are delivered to a shop with a delivery note, not an invoice. After thirty days the publisher should call with the shop and establish how many copies have sold. If they have sold out, an invoice for the total quantity should be issued at that point and, with any luck, the manager will order another quantity on the same basis. If on the other hand some copies have remained unsold, the publisher and manager should decide whether they can remain on the shelves for another month or whether the publisher should take back the unsold copies and issue an invoice for the sold copies.

Where an Eason shop has decided to order your book, it makes sense to develop a good relationship with the manager and staff and to keep an eye on the stock level – remember to avoid over-pushiness and to keep your approach friendly and helpful.

Selling to Waterstone's

Waterstone's have five retail bookshops in Northern Ireland and their buyers are very much geared to dealing with representatives from larger publishers, wholesalers and distributors. However, the company currently has two methods for dealing with new/small publishers, both run by the Irish commercial manager, Alyson Wilson. She is based at the Fountain Street branch in Belfast, and should be contacted in the first instance *by email only* at alyson.wilson@waterstones.com – she regrets that she doesn't have time to see people who make a cold call.

The first method is the Community Activity Account which is intended for one-off publications that are of particular interest to a local Waterstone's branch. If interested, Alyson Wilson will order such titles on a firm-sale basis and says she 'can be flexible on discount, particularly if it is a charity book'. The second method, the Small Supplier Account, is more difficult – it allows small publishers to open new accounts with Waterstone's, but only if they have first obtained representation through one of the Irish book distributors like Gill & Macmillan, CMD or Argosy. In addition, Alyson Wilson says she will 'in exceptional circumstances' allow a small publisher to open an account directly with Waterstone's, but she warns that the terms are tough – 50 per cent discount, fully sale-or-return terms and ninety days credit.

Selling to libraries

Northern Irish libraries obtain their books from a variety of sources, including local booksellers and specialist library suppliers in Northern Ireland, the Republic of Ireland and Great Britain. Your sales approach to libraries needs to be two-pronged: to the libraries themselves and to their suppliers. Send your advance information sheet to all the libraries you think would be interested – to the librarian in the case of smaller libraries and to the local studies librarian in the larger ones. (The website address for Northern Ireland libraries is www.ni-libraries.net.) At the same time, send the sheet to booksellers and library suppliers: you'll find a list of them in the 'Directory of useful publishing resources' at the back of this book. There is no standard discounting system – if you are sent an order from a library supplier it will probably specify an expected discount level, but it's worthwhile trying to negotiate this down if you're uncomfortable with it.

Many librarians welcome publishers using their libraries as venues for launches, talks and readings – this is a promotional opportunity that you should grab with both hands.

of delivery). Where possible, get an order in writing – there is nothing worse than an oral promise that mysteriously fades away come delivery time.

Your attitude during sales calls is all-important. Naturally, you should be enthusiastic and positive about the book but always treat buyers and their colleagues with politeness. Put yourself in their shoes: try to foresee reasons why they might be reluctant to stock your book and be ready to counter them in a pleasant manner. It's galling to be dismissed with a small order or even none at all, but losing your cool is counter-productive as well as unprofessional.

Trading terms

DISCOUNTS   In general, independent booksellers will expect a discount of at least 35 per cent off the retail price, and, as outlined earlier, bookselling chains like Eason and Waterstone's will want to impose their own terms. Other outlets like village shops etc will probably not have a sct discount for books as they are not their normal stock-in-trade, but you could offer, say, 25 per cent and be prepared to go higher (always within your budget, of course).

If you would like your book to be sold online by Amazon, you should be prepared to give them around 60 per cent off the retail price. Contact them via their website www.amazon.co.uk and also consider joining their Advantage Scheme – see www.amazon.co.uk/advantage.

LENGTH OF CREDIT   In the book trade, the notional standard for length of credit is thirty days from invoice, generally interpreted to mean the last day of the month following the month of the invoice date. Do remember that larger chains routinely take more than this – often up to ninety days or more. On the other hand, a small shop like a newsagent may be prepared to pay cash on delivery, perhaps for a slight increase in discount, but this is comparatively rare.

RETURNED BOOKS   Painful as it seems, book-trade custom accepts that booksellers can return unsold books ('returns') and receive back the price they paid for them provided they are in resaleable condition. If possible, avoid selling on a sale-or-return basis, by which the publisher receives no payment at all until the bookseller either sells all the books or returns unsold ones. The retail book trade usually works on a 'see-safe' basis, which means that the publisher gets paid for the full consignment within an agreed time and then, if there are subsequently any books returned in a resaleable condition, reimburses the bookseller for them. On the other

Direct sales

Many small and some not-so-small publishers avoid the problem of high trade discounts by selling directly to the public. This can be done the old-fashioned way by mailshot, where potential customers are sent an attractive flyer about the forthcoming book along with an order form inviting them to reserve a copy or copies, usually on a money-up-front basis. Properly planned and costed, this can be an effective sales method – the publisher gets a better feel of likely sales and sensible print runs, receives a higher proportion of the retail price and doesn't have a long wait for payment. It also gives the publisher room to offer incentives to the customer in the form of free post and packaging and/or a small discount.

Some publishers now sell directly via the Internet, having set up their own websites and ordering systems. It is probably best to pay an IT expert to do this for you, unless you are really confident that you can deal with issues like customer security during credit card transactions etc. Small publishers can sometimes hitch a ride on the websites of other publishers – for example, in Northern Ireland the Ulster Historical Foundation and the Ultach Trust will occasionally include details of books from other publishers on their online selling sites if they are felt to be compatible with their own publications.

Selling by subscription

In the eighteenth and nineteenth centuries, many books were sold by subscription, i.e. a number of people reserved a copy of a forthcoming book by paying the publisher for it in advance; in return, they would often have their names displayed in a list of subscribers at the end of the book. Although rare, this method is still occasionally used – it might work well with, say, a history of a golf club, with members invited to become subscribers. An attractive and informative flyer should be distributed to likely subscribers, with an order form setting out the price plus any post and packaging costs (you might decide that because you are not having to offer a discount you can afford to offer free p & p). While selling by subscription would certainly be one way to get around the usual cash-flow problem of production bills having to be paid before any sales income is received, it would of course entail keeping a meticulous record of subscriptions and ensuring that subscribers' names were included in the printed list and that they received their copies in pristine condition immediately they were printed.

hand, wholesalers like Eason insist on dealing on a sale-or-return basis and if you want your books to be in their shops you really have no option but to comply.

Distribution

First things first: as soon as you receive your consignment of multiple copies from the printer, store them carefully in a clean, dry place with some low background heat – the slightest hint of damp will cause paper to swell and warp, making books unsaleable.

After sending the author the agreed number of free copies, the next priority is to despatch review copies to targeted media with all haste, together with an eye-catching press release and any extra material such as author photographs. Send the books and information in padded envelopes to the individual journalists you have already identified as most appropriate for your book. While it's important to generate media attention, put a sensible limit on the number of review copies you send – as well as costing money to post, every free copy represents potential lost income.

Now turn your attention to fulfilling collected orders. You should have systematically filed all advance orders as they came in. Go through them and prepare invoices and/or delivery notes, carefully following any instructions from the customer regarding order number etc. Make up the orders, ideally using robust cardboard boxes and plenty of packaging to stop the books sliding about and getting scuffed. Don't forget to include the invoice and/or delivery note and add 'INVOICE ENCLOSED' to the address on the outside of the box. Also remember to include any previously ordered point-of-sale material like posters and bookmarks. If there are multiple boxes in an order, clearly mark them '1 of 4', '2 of 4' etc.

Local orders can be delivered from a car boot or a borrowed van. If you have time, deliver them yourself and seize the opportunity for a cheery word with the staff as you unload. By the way, it's worth checking that busy booksellers are actually unpacking your consignments and setting the books out on the shelves, and that wholesalers aren't delaying in distributing copies to their outlets.

For more distant deliveries, use the post or a delivery service, having worked out in advance which is more cost-effective. Use good quality padded envelopes for individual books, remembering to enclose an invoice, or a delivery note if the customer has paid already.

Once you have despatched author copies, review copies and customer orders, your next job is the distribution of free copies. These include legal deposit copies and copies (if stipulated) to anyone who has given permission to use copyright material. You may also want to present a few copies to local celebrities or people of influence, thus creating photo-opportunities that will raise the profile of the book. Finally, if you are publishing in Northern Ireland, don't forget to send two copies to NIPR, the Northern Ireland Publications Resource.

Follow-up sales

Let's assume that your publicity and sales campaign turns out to be more successful than you could have dreamed and that your book starts to sell really well. Don't sit waiting for booksellers to phone in re-orders – with so many other books in the shops, they may not even have noticed that your pile of copies was diminishing. Have a look in bookshops and other outlets yourself and if your book appears to be out of stock or approaching that state, politely suggest a re-order. Drop into the conversation any interesting news about the book. If it has had rave reviews, show the cuttings. Again, good humour and good manners will get you further than petulance and over-pushiness. Keep your temper even if you are not getting the response you think your book deserves

Sales accounting

Make sure that your invoices are clear and user-friendly, with your details prominently displayed as well as the customer's order date and number. The invoice should show delivery date, book title, quantity delivered, discount applied and net amount owed, as well as the required payment date. At each month's end, send a statement presenting a detailed list of all invoices still owing and follow it up with a phone call if you feel that any payments are overdue.

Don't be embarrassed to chase money owed to you – there's no need to be aggressive, but you will often need to be assertive to get to the top of a customer's 'issue payment' list. Cash-flow problems are especially prevalent in publishing, where printing and other bills have to be paid long before a book's sales income is received and it's crucial that you narrow this financial gap as much as possible.

Legal deposit copies

Publishers in the UK and Ireland have a **legal requirement** to send one copy of each of their publications to the Legal Deposit Office of the British Library within one month of publication. In addition, the Universities of Oxford and Cambridge, the National Library of Scotland, the Library of Trinity College Dublin and the National Library of Wales have the right to request one copy each; these can be supplied via the Agency for the Legal Deposit Libraries in London (see 'Directory of useful publishing resources').

Publishers in Northern Ireland are also requested to donate two copies of each publication to Northern Ireland Publications Resource (NIPR). (See inside front cover of this book for address details.)

and remember the buyer is used to every publisher insisting their latest book is the greatest thing since Harry Potter.

If sales are really booming, you may have to consider ordering a reprint. Bear in mind that sales can tail off as well as gallop and don't get too carried away in the heat of the moment. The weeks before Christmas are especially dangerous here. Because your book is flying out of the shops at the beginning of December and the shops are putting in big re-orders, the temptation is to place an order for a large reprint. But printing takes time and even the most accommodating printer may be chock-a-block with seasonal work for other publishers. As a result, your reprint may not arrive in the shops until a few days before Christmas, too late for most of them to be sold before the rush stops. Even the most experienced publishers have found themselves with mountains of returned books in January and facing a large printer's bill for a reprint that has turned out to be unnecessary.

However, you may have a real runaway bestseller on your hands, with bookshops and the public clamouring for copies and no time constraints (like the Christmas scenario mentioned above) to worry you. In that case, it's happy days for you and the author, provided you keep a cool head as you order reprints, generate extra publicity, collect new orders from the shops and achieve fast turnaround times for those orders when the reprinted books are delivered.

Remaindering

If the worst comes to the worst and you are left with a quantity of books that isn't shifting in spite of your best efforts, or is even increasing because booksellers are returning unsold copies, then it's time to consider selling them off at a reduced price. It's good practice to give authors first refusal in these cases: it can save them the embarrassment of seeing their books marked down and they may well be content to have a stockpile of copies they can distribute as gifts or sell at talks and readings over a period of years.

After the author, talk to the booksellers and wholesalers you have been dealing with and try to negotiate some special deals – some bookshops may have seasonal sales, for instance, and be willing to add your book to the 'special offer' table. Another possibility is to approach those bookshops that specialise in bargain books.

With all of these outlets, be prepared for tough bargaining as the booksellers will want the books at a very low price. It's up to you whether or not to accept their terms, but bear in mind that it's probably better to have the unsold stock generating *some* financial return for you rather than gently mouldering away somewhere.

In conclusion

As I said at the outset, publishing can be both frustrating and rewarding. I hope that this book will help to eliminate some of the frustrations and enhance the some of the rewards for you. It doesn't pretend to be comprehensive – publishing is far too complex and dynamic for that to be achieved in such a slim volume. Nor is it intended to be prescriptive – there are as many ways to publish books as there are publishers.

The tips and suggestions presented in the previous chapters are based on long experience and on numerous conversations with other publishers over the years. There is a tradition of co-operation among Irish publishers that sometimes surprises publishers from other countries – it arose from the fact that most Irish publishing houses operating today were founded in the 1970s and weren't able to rely on a settled tradition or an inherited set of publishing systems. We had to make it up as we went along, and comparing notes with each other became a lifeline for many of us.

If you are a new publisher, remember that this tradition of co-operation still exists and that most publishers will be prepared to share their experience and expertise with you. You may get the odd dusty answer, or a publisher may simply be too busy to speak to you just at that moment (don't make the classic mistake of approaching a publisher at a book launch when he or she is frenetically busy) but as the saying goes, if you don't ask, you won't get.

We hope that becoming a publisher will turn out to be one of the most interesting things you've ever done and we're greatly looking forward to seeing a new wave of local books that not only look confident and professional, but are backed by imaginative publicity and effective sales and distribution.

Good luck!

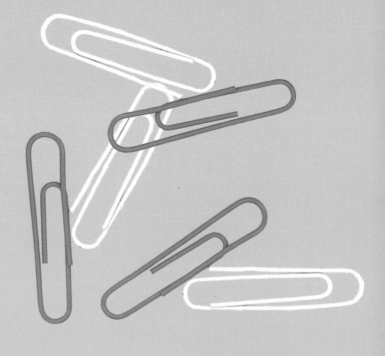

Appendices

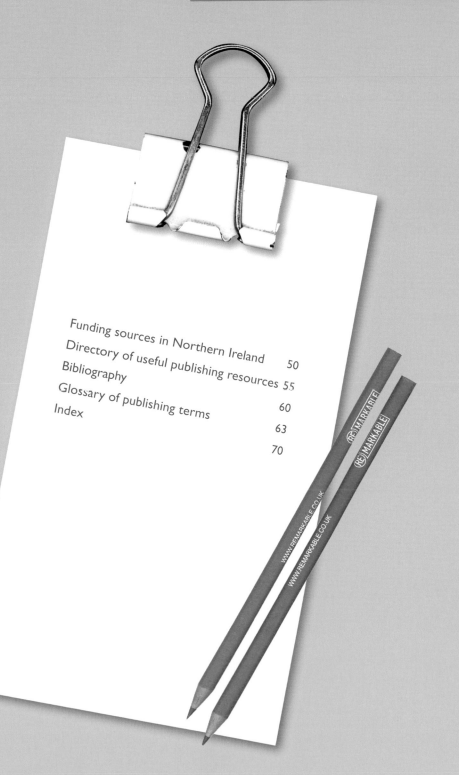

Before you undertake any publishing venture you must consider the high costs entailed. If you decide to try for external funding to help you with production costs, you should bear in mind that getting financial backing for any Northern Ireland publication is very difficult, as there is only a limited number of grants available and competition for these is high. In addition, the application procedures can be quite time-consuming, so you need to factor that into your schedule. Here is a list of possible funding sources.

Local councils

At present local administration in Northern Ireland is carried out through twenty-six local councils (although this may change in the near future). Each council is keen to promote culture and arts in their own area and the majority have employed dedicated arts officers to ensure this happens. Many *but not all* councils offer small grants to publishers who are producing publications about the culture or heritage of the local district. To find out if your council offers any such funding schemes you should contact the local arts officer.

COUNCIL	WEBSITE	PHONE (028 +)
Antrim Borough Council	www.antrim.gov.uk	9448 1338
Ards Borough Council	www.ards-council.gov.uk	9181 0803
Armagh City and District Council	www.armagh.gov.uk	3752 1820
Ballymena Borough Council	www.ballymena.gov.uk	2563 9853
Ballymoney Borough Council	www.ballymoney.gov.uk	2766 0229
Banbridge District Council	www.banbridge.com	4066 0632
Belfast City Council	www.belfastcity.gov.uk	9027 0229
Carrickfergus Borough Council	www.carrickfergus.org	9335 8042
Castlereagh Borough Council	www.castlereagh.gov.uk	9049 4566
Coleraine Borough Council	www.colerainebc.gov.uk	7083 1400
Cookstown District Council	www.cookstown.gov.uk	8676 2205
Craigavon Borough Council	www.craigavon.gov.uk	3831 1680
Derry City Council	www.derrycity.gov.uk	7136 5151
Down District Council	www.downdc.gov.uk	4461 5283
Dungannon & S. Tyrone Council	www.dungannon.gov.uk	8775 3626

Fermanagh Council	www.fermanagh.gov.uk	6632 5050
Larne Council	www.larne.gov.uk	2827 0824
Limavady Council	www.limavady.gov.uk	7776 0304
Lisburn Council	www.lisburn.gov.uk	9250 9509
Magherafelt District Council	www.magherafelt.gov.uk	7963 2151
Moyle District Council	www.moyle-council.org	2076 2225
Newry & Mourne District Council	www.newryandmourne.gov.uk	3031 3180
Newtownabbey Borough Council	www.newtownabbey.gov.uk	9034 0063
North Down Borough Council	www.northdown.gov.uk	9127 8032
Omagh District Council	www.omagh.gov.uk	8224 5321
Strabane District Council	www.strabanedc.com	7138 2204

Arts Council of Northern Ireland

The Arts Council of Northern Ireland offers a wide range of funding opportunities through their exchequer and National Lottery Funds. If your organisation is applying for a grant of up to £10,000, you need to contact Awards for All (see below). If, however, you require more substantial funding, you should contact:

The Arts Council of Northern Ireland
77 Malone Road
Belfast, BT9 6AQ
PHONE: 028 9038 5200
WEB: www.artscouncil-ni.org

Awards for All Northern Ireland

Awards for All Northern Ireland is supported by the Big Lottery, the Heritage Lottery Fund, the Arts Council of Northern Ireland and the Sports Council of Northern Ireland. It offers awards of between £500 and £10,000 to non-profit-making organisations. One of its aims is 'to bring people together and increase community activity', which of course can be achieved by recording people's memories, producing a local history or celebrating a significant anniversary through the medium of print. For further information contact:

Awards for All
1 Cromac Quay
Cromac Wood
Ormeau Road
Belfast, BT7 2JD
PHONE: 028 9055 9090
WEB: www.awardsforall.org.uk/northernireland/

Belfast Society, The

The Belfast Society will consider applications for financial assistance with publications relating specifically to Irish historical studies. The society will assess each application, and grants of up to approximately £1,500 are available. In return, publishers must acknowledge the society in the publication and give the society two copies.

For further information contact:

Treasurer
The Belfast Society
c/o Linen Hall Library
17 Donegall Square North
Belfast, BT1 5GB
PHONE: 028 9032 1707
WEB: www.belfastsociety.com

Bord na Leabhar Gaeilge/Foras na Gaeilge

Publishers seeking funding to assist in the publication of Irish-language books should in the first instance contact Bord na Leabhar Gaeilge. All the contact details are available on their website www.leabhar.ie. Where Bord na Leabhar Gaeilge is unable to assist, Foras na Gaeilge can consider an application for part-sponsorship for a book in Irish or a book related to cultural aspects of the Irish language. For further information contact:

Foras na Gaeilge
Westgate House
2–4 Queen Street
Belfast, BT1 6ED
PHONE: 028 9089 0970
WEB: www.gaeilge.ie

Community Foundation for Northern Ireland

The Community Foundation for Northern Ireland manages a number of funds which aim to tackle poverty, social inclusion and social injustice. The Telecommunity Programme, in conjunction with BT, provides grants of up to £1,000 to community-based organisations in socially disadvantaged areas which work with older people, teenagers and people with disabilities. For further information contact:

Community Foundation for Northern Ireland
Citylink Business Park
Albert Street
Belfast, BT12 4HQ
PHONE: 028 9024 5927
WEB: www.communityfoundationni.org

Community Relations Council

The Community Relations Council (CRC) offers financial support and advice to projects run by community or voluntary groups that have a community relations purpose or value. The Publications Grant Scheme awards grants of up to £7,000 and it aims 'to encourage the production and dissemination of publications that will contribute to greater understanding and better community relations in Northern Ireland'. For further information contact:

> **Community Relations Council**
> 6 Murray Street
> Belfast, BT1 6DW
> PHONE: 028 9022 7500
> WEB: www.community-relations.org.uk

Esmé Mitchell Trust

The Esmé Mitchell Trust is particulary interested in assisting charitable projects in Northern Ireland, with a particular emphasis on cultural or artistic endeavours. Individuals cannot apply. For further information contact:

> **Esmé Mitchell Trust**
> Northern Bank Executor & Trustee Co. Ltd
> PO Box 183
> Donegall Square West
> Belfast, BT1 6JS
> PHONE: 028 9024 5277
> WEB: n/a

Support for Local Studies Publication Policy –
North Eastern Education & Library Board

The NEELB's 'Support for Local Studies Publication Policy' is intended to encourage the publication of material relating to the history of the region it covers. It awards grants of £250 (three per year) to help towards printing and publication costs. For further information contact:

> **Library Headquarters**
> NEELB
> Demesne Avenue
> Ballymena, BT43 7BQ
> PHONE: 028 2566 4100
> WEB: www.neelb.org.uk

Ulster Garden Villages

Ulster Garden Villages 'primarily allocates funds to projects within

Northern Ireland that will have a positive impact in Northern Ireland'. In addition to outright grants, financial assistance may be given by way of loans which may carry certain conditions at the discretion of the committee. Individuals may not apply but there is no restriction on the amount that can be applied for. For further information contact:

Ulster Garden Villages Ltd
'Forestview'
Purdy's Lane
Newtownbreda
Belfast, BT8 7AR
PHONE: 028 9049 1111
WEB: www.ulstergardenvillages.co.uk

Ulster Local History Trust

The Ulster Local History Trust aims to raise the standard of local historical work by giving financial assistance and advice to local history societies throughout Northern Ireland. Grants of up to £3,000 are available. For further information contact:

Ulster Local History Trust
PO Box 900
Downpatrick, BT30 6EF
PHONE: n/a
WEB: www.ulht.org

Ulster-Scots Agency

The Ulster-Scots Agency aims to promote the conservation, development, study and use of Ulster-Scots as a living language. The agency runs a financial assistance scheme with grants available to promote a 'greater awareness and use of Ullans and Ulster-Scots cultural issues, both within Northern Ireland and throughout the island'. There is no restriction on the amount that can be applied for. For further information contact:

Ulster-Scots Agency
5th Floor, Franklin House
10–12 Brunswick Street
Belfast, BT2 7GE
PHONE: 028 9032 1113
WEB: www.ulsterscotsagency.com

Directory of useful publishing resources

Publishing Associations

Clé: The Irish Book Publishers' Association
25 Denzille Lane
Dublin 2
PHONE: 003531 639 4868
WEB: www.publishingireland.com

Scottish Publishers Association
Scottish Book Centre
137 Dundee Street
Edinburgh, EH11 1BG
PHONE: 0131 228 6866
WEB: www.scottishbooks.org

Independent Publishers Guild
PO Box 93
Royston, SG8 5GH
PHONE: 01763 247 014
WEB: www.ipg.uk.com

Publishers Association
29b Montague Street
London, WC1B 5BW
PHONE: 020 7691 9191
WEB: www.publishers.org.uk

Periodical Publishers Association
Queen's House
28 Kingsway, London, WC2B 6JR
PHONE: 020 7404 4166
WEB: www.ppa.co.uk

Society of Publishers in Ireland
WEB: www.the-spi.com

Training courses

Clé: The Irish Book Publishers' Association
25 Denzille Lane
Dublin 2
PHONE: 003531 639 4868
WEB: www.publishingireland.com

Scottish Publishers Association
Scottish Book Centre
137 Dundee Street
Edinburgh, EH11 1BG
PHONE: 0131 228 6866
WEB: www.scottishbooks.org

Publishing Training Centre at Bookhouse
45 East Hill
Wandsworth, London, SW18 2QZ
PHONE: 020 8870 8985
WEB: www.train4publishing.co.uk

Society for Editors and Proofreaders
Riverbank House
1 Putney Bridge Approach
Fulham, London, SW6 3JD
PHONE: 020 7736 3278
WEB: www.sfep.org.uk

Publishing Skills Group
South House
The Street
Clapham, Worthing,
West Sussex, BN13 3UU
PHONE: 01903 871 686
WEB: www.publishingskills.org.uk

Freelance editors' associations

Association of Freelance Editors, Proofreaders, Indexers [Ireland]
www.afepi.ie

Society for Freelance Editors and Proofreaders
Riverbank House
1 Putney Bridge Approach
Fulham, London, SW6 3JD
PHONE: 020 7736 3278
WEB: www.sfep.org.uk

Society of Indexers
Woodburn Business Centre
10 Jessell Street
Sheffield, S9 3HY
PHONE: 0114 244 9561
WEB: www.indexers.org.uk

Freelance editorial services in NI

The following list gives a selection only. NIPR does not endorse any one individual or company and other names may be found from directories and internet searches.

Hilary Bell
51 Shore Road
Strangford, BT30 7NW
PHONE: 028 4488 1575
EMAIL: hilarybelleditor@btinternet.com

Averill Buchanan
4 Woodburn Drive
Belfast, BT15 5FR
PHONE: 07875 857 278
EMAIL: averill@averillbuchanan.com

Editorial Solutions
537 Antrim Road
Belfast, BT15 3BU
PHONE: 028 9077 2300
EMAIL: info@editorialsolutions.com

Joan Erskine
9 Knocklofty Park
Belfast, BT4 3NA
PHONE: 028 9065 7810
EMAIL: jmerskine@btinternet.com

Feldstein Agency
47a Princetown Road
Bangor, BT20 3TA
PHONE: 028 9146 2662
EMAIL: susan@thefeldsteinagency.co.uk

Linda Houston
26 Glenkeen,
Randalstown, BT41 3JX
PHONE: 028 9447 2874
EMAIL: linda.houston2@btinternet.com

Beth Humphries
44 Hopefield Avenue,
Portrush, BT56 8HB
PHONE: 028 7082 1428
EMAIL: beth@b.humphries.bbmax.co.uk

Marnie Kennedy
42 Indiana Avenue
Belfast, BT15 5BZ
PHONE: 028 9077 3560
EMAIL: marnie.kennedy@talktalk.net

Anne Loughran
211a Cavehill Road
Belfast, BT15 5BQ
PHONE: 028 9072 9353
WEB: www.apjpublications.co.uk

Alexandra McKee
Word Works
32 Mullaghbane Road
Greystone
Dungannon, BT70 1SR
PHONE: 028 8772 5628
EMAIL: wordworks@fastmail.fm

Helen Roberts
2 Dalton Park
Comber, BT23 5HD
PHONE: 028 9187 8983
EMAIL: helen_roberts@dsl.pipex.com

Anne Tannahill
71 Glenburn Road
Dunmurry, BT17 9AN
PHONE: 028 9061 7340
EMAIL: anne@tannahill71.fsnet.co.uk

Designers in NI

The following list gives a selection only. NIPR does not endorse any one individual or company and other names may be found from directories and internet searches.

Alexander Design
7 Loughbrin Park
Carryduff
Belfast, BT8 8PL
PHONE: 07759 545754
EMAIL: info@alexanderdesign-ni.com

April Sky Design
Jubilee Business Park, 21 Jubilee Road
Newtownards, BT23 4HY
PHONE: 028 9182 7195
EMAIL: wesley@aprilsky.co.uk

Atto
1 Exchange Place
Belfast, BT1 2NA
PHONE: 028 9027 8338
EMAIL: karys@helloatto.com

Michael Beggs
6 Hawthornden Gardens
Belfast, BT4 2HF
PHONE: 07912 060 081
EMAIL: michaelwbeggs@hotmail.com

Dunbar Design
11 My Lady's Mile
Holywood, BT18 9EW
PHONE: 028 9042 2055
EMAIL: dunbar.design@ntlworld.com

Flixx Graphics
30 Irish Street
Downpatrick, BT51 2GG
PHONE: 028 4461 5613
EMAIL: info@flixxgraphics.com

Graphic Base
Unit A6, Ards Business Centre
Jubilee Road
Newtownards, BT23 4YH
PHONE: 028 9182 1810
EMAIL: info@graphicbase.co.uk

Postcard Company
51 Gortin Road
Omagh, BT79 7HZ
PHONE: 028 8224 9222
EMAIL: sales@thepostcardcompany.com

Joan Shannon
41a Newal Road
Ballymoney, BT53 6HB
PHONE: 028 2766 2953
EMAIL: joan@joanshannon.co.uk

Tenpoint Design
27b Main Street
Kircubbin, BT22 2SS
PHONE: 028 4273 8585
EMAIL: info@tenpointdesign.com

Zing Design & Print
Loughanhill Industrial Estate
Gateside Road
Coleraine, BT52 2NR
PHONE: 028 7034 2472
EMAIL: info@zingdp.com

Printers in NI

The following list gives a selection only.
NIPR does not endorse any one company
and other names may be found from
directories and internet searches.

Action Press
Unit 15/16 Down Business Park
46 Belfast Road
Downpatrick, BT30 9UP
PHONE: 028 4483 9090
WEB: www.actionpress.co.uk

W & G Baird
Greystone Road
Antrim, BT41 2RS
PHONE: 028 9446 3911
WEB: www.wgbaird.com

Dorman & Sons
Unit 2, Apollo Road
Belfast, BT12 6HP
PHONE: 028 9066 6700
WEB: www.dormans-print.co.uk

Graham & Heslip
96 Beechill Road
Belfast, BT8 7QN
PHONE: 028 9049 4949
WEB: www.ghprint.com

Impact Printing
Leyland Road
Ballycastle, BT54 6EZ
PHONE: 028 2076 2469
WEB: www.impactpublishers.co.uk

Nicholson & Bass
3 Nicholson Drive
Newtownabbey, BT36 4FB
PHONE: 028 9034 2433
WEB: www.nicholsonbass.com

Peninsula Print and Design
Unit 4 & 5 North Road Business Park
Quarry Heights
Newtownards, BT23 7SZ
PHONE: 028 9181 4125
WEB: www.peninsulaprint.co.uk

Print Factory Printers
Lackaghboy Industrial Estate
Tempo Road
Enniskillen, BT47 4RL
PHONE: 028 6632 6960
WEB: www.theprintfactory.com

Writers' Societies

Creative Writers' Network
109–113 Royal Avenue
Belfast, BT1 1FF
PHONE: 028 9031 2361
WEB: www.creativewritersnetwork.org

Irish Writers' Centre
19 Parnell Square
Dublin 1
PHONE: 003531 872 1302
WEB: www.writerscentre.ie

Irish Writers' Union
19 Parnell Square
Dublin 1
PHONE: 003531 872 1302
WEB: www.ireland-writers.com

Bookselling

Eason
EMAIL: rgourley@easonwholesale.com

Waterstone's
EMAIL: alyson.wilson@waterstones.com

Booksellers Association
Minister House
272 Vauxhall Bridge Road
London, SW1V 1BA
PHONE: 020 7802 0802
WEB: www.booksellers.org.uk

Library suppliers in NI

Eason
20 Donegall Place
Belfast, BT1 5BA
PHONE: 028 9023 5070
WEB: www.easons.com

Bookshop at Queen's
91 University Rd
Belfast, BT7 1NL
PHONE: 028 9066 2552
WEB: www.queensbookshop.co.uk

Rondo
Rondo House
Dundonald Enterprise Park
Carrowreagh Road
Dundonald
Belfast, BT16 1QT
PHONE: 028 9048 1100
WEB: www.rondo.co.uk

Smyth & Ryan
Church Lodge
Moneyreagh
Newtownards, BT23 6EX
PHONE: 028 9044 8333

Waterstone's Booksellers
44–46 Fountain St
Belfast, BT1 5EE
PHONE: 028 9024 0159
WEB: www.waterstones.co.uk

Library suppliers outside NI

Amazon   www.amazon.co.uk
Argosy   www.argosybooks.ie
Askews   www.askews.co.uk
Book Nest   www.booknest.ie
Dawson's Books   www.dawsonbooks.co.uk
Holt Jackson   www.holtjackson.co.uk

Legal Deposit/Copyright/ISBN

Agency for the Legal Deposit Libraries
100 Euston Street
London, NW1 2HQ
PHONE: 020 7388 5061
WEB: www.llgc.org.uk/aldl/

British Library
Boston Spa
Wetherby
West Yorkshire, LS23 7BY
PHONE: 0193 754 6268
WEB: www.bl.uk

Northern Ireland Publications Resource (NIPR)
See inside front cover for address details

Bibliographic Data Services Limited
Publishers Liaison Department
Annandale House
The Crichton
Dumfries, DG1 4TA
PHONE: 0387 702 251
WEB: www.bibliographicdata.com

Copyright Licensing Agency
Saffron House
610 Kirby Road
London, EC1N 8TS
PHONE: 020 7400 3100
WEB: www.cla.org.uk

UK ISBN Agency
Nielsen Bookdata
3rd Floor, Midas House
62 Goldsworth Road
Woking, GU21 6LQ
PHONE: 0870 777 8710
WEB: www.isbn.nielsenbookdata.co.uk

Other Resources (Online)

Association of Freelance Editors, Proofreaders, Indexers   www.afepi.ie
Authors Online   www.authorsonline.co.uk
Author.co.uk   www.author.co.uk
Bookseller magazine   www.thebookseller.com
Go Publish Yourself   www.go-publish-yourself.com
How to Publish Yourself in the UK www.publish-yourself.com
Lulu (Print on demand)   www.lulu.com
Proofreading & Copy-editing   www.copyediting.co.uk
Publishing Central   www.publishingcentral.com
Publishing News   www.publishingnews.co.uk
Self Published Authors Forum   www.selfpublishedauthors.com
Society of Young Publishers   www.thesyp.org.uk
Unlimited Publishing   www.unlimitedpublishing.com
Vanity Publishing   www.vanitypublishing.info
Women in Publishing   www.wipub.org.uk
Writers World   www.writersworld.co.uk

Bibliography

While this bibliography is by no means comprehensive, you may find the following titles useful.

Financial management

KOGAN, PHILIP & WOLL, THOMAS. *Publishing for Profit: Successful Bottom-line Management for Book Publishers.* London: Kogan Page, 1999. ISBN 978074929409

Legal aspects

BENSON, CHRISTOPHER & JONES, HUGH. *Publishing Law.* London: Routledge, 2006. ISBN 9780415384278

CORNISH, GRAHAM. *Copyright: Interpreting the Law for Libraries, Archives and Information Services.* London: Facet Publishing, 2004. ISBN 978-1856045087

LEGAT, MICHAEL. *Understanding Publishers' Contracts.* London: Robert Hale, 2002. ISBN 9780709072898

OWEN, LYNETTE (ed.). *Clark's Publishing Agreements: A Book of Precedents.* Haywards Heath: Tottel Publishing, 2007. ISBN 9781845927851

PADFIELD, TIM. *Copyright for Record Managers and Archivists.* London: Facet Publishing, 2007. ISBN 9781856046046

WALL, RAYMOND *et al. Copyright Made Easier.* London: Europa Publications, 2000. ISBN 9780851424477

Preparing the text (editing & indexing)

BROWNE, GLENDA & JERMEY, JON. *The Indexing Companion.* Cambridge: Cambridge University Press, 2007. ISBN 9780521689885

BUTCHER, JUDITH, DRAKE, CAROLINE & LEACH, MAUREEN. *Butcher's Copy-editing: The Cambridge Handbook for Editors, Copy-editors and Proofreaders.* Cambridge: Cambridge University Press, 2006. ISBN 9780521847131

The Chicago Manual of Style: For Authors, Editors and Copywriters. Chicago and London: University of Chicago Press, 2003. ISBN 9780226104034

MANSER, MARTIN & CURTIS, STEPHEN. *The Penguin Writer's Manual.* London: Penguin Books, 2002. ISBN 9780140514896

RITTER, R.M. (ed.). *New Hart's Rules: The Handbook of Style for Writers and Editors.* Oxford: Oxford University Press, 2005. ISBN 9780198610410

RITTER, R.M. (ed.) *New Oxford Dictionary for Writers and Editors: The Essential A–Z Guide to the Written Word.* Oxford: Oxford University Press, 2005. ISBN 9780198610403

RITTER, R.M. (ed.). *Oxford Style Manual.* Oxford: Oxford University Press, 2003. ISBN 9780198605645

TRASK, R.L. *The Penguin Guide to Punctuation.* London: Penguin Books, 1997. ISBN 9780140513660

Production
(design, typesetting & printing)

BARTRAM, ALAN. *Creating the Printed Page: A Guide for Authors, Publishers and Designers.* London: British Library, 2006. ISBN 9780712346962

BHASKARAN, LAKSHMI. *What is Publication Design?* London: Rotovision, 2007. ISBN 9782940361465

GATTER, MARK. *Software Essentials for Graphic Designers.* London: Laurence King Publishing, 2006. ISBN 9781856694995

HASLAM, ANDREW. *Book Design.* London: Laurence King Publishing, 2006. ISBN 9781856694735

Marketing

BAVERSTOCK, ALISON. *Marketing Your Book: An Author's Guide.* London: A & C Black, 2001. ISBN 9780713659658

BLYTHE, J. *Essentials of Marketing.* Harlow: Prentice Hall, 2005. ISBN 9780273702054

CADY, MICHAEL. *Writer's Market UK 2008.* Newton Abbott: David & Charles, 2007. ISBN 9780715326619

Self-publishing

ANTHONY, JOANNA. *What Do I Have to Do to Get a Book Published? The Essential Guide to Self-Publishing in the UK.* Brighton: Pen Press, 2006. ISBN 9781905203581

CROSBIE, ANNA. *How to Publish Your Own Book: Everything You Need to Know About the Self- Publishing Process.* Oxford: How to Books, 2006. ISBN 9781845281069

McCALLUM, CHRIS. *The Beginner's Guide to Getting Published.* Oxford: How to Books, 2003. ISBN 9781845282172

OLIVER, MARINA. *Write and Sell Your Novel. The Beginner's Guide to Writing for Publishers.* Oxford: How to Books, 2003. ISBN 9781857038767

ROWSON, PAULINE. *The Easy Step by Step Guide to Publishing and Promoting Your Book.* Hayling Island: Rowmark, 2006. ISBN 9781857038767

STOCK, RACHAEL. *The Insider's Guide to Getting Your Book Published.* Great Ambrook: White Ladder Press, 2005. ISBN 9780954821951

General Reference

Booksellers Association. *Directory of Publishing 2008 (UK and the Republic of Ireland)*. London: Continuum International Publishing Group, 2007. ISBN 9780826499271

Dictionary of Printing and Publishing. London: A & C Black, 2006. ISBN 9780713675894

Directory of Publishing in Scotland. Edinburgh: Scottish Publishers Association, 2007. ISBN 9780954865757

GLAISTER, GEOFFREY. *Glaister's Glossary of the Book*. London: Allen & Unwin, 1980. ISBN 9780040100069

TURNER, BARRY (ed.). *The Writer's Handbook 2008*. London: Macmillan, 2007. ISBN 9780230016378

Writers' & Artists' Yearbook 2008. London: A & C Black, 2007. ISBN 9780713683714

acknowledgements
a statement, usually printed at the beginning of a book, expressing the author's or publisher's gratitude to others for help or ideas, and/or for permission to use copyright material

appendix (appendices)
a section at the end of a book presenting subsidiary material

artwork
1 non-textual material e.g. illustrations, photographs, maps etc, *or*
2 typeset material presented to a printer in electronic form

bibliography
a list of books or other texts referred to in a book or containing related material

bleed
an illustration printed so that it runs off a trimmed page, leaving no margin

blurb
a short promotional description of a book, printed on the front flap of a hardback or the back cover of a paperback

Cataloguing-in-Publication (CIP)
a process whereby the British Library creates a catalogue record for books not yet published, based on the details supplied by the publisher

copy
raw text prior to copy-editing

copy-editing
preparing a text for typesetting by correcting errors, checking for consistency etc

copyright
a property right belonging to the creator of a work, e.g. the author of a text, who may exclusively license it to e.g. a publisher under certain agreed conditions

cropping
removing unwanted parts of illustrations

dedication
an inscription printed near the beginning of a book in which the author dedicates the work to a named individual or individuals

displayed quote/quotation
quoted material that is differentiated from the main text by being displayed with an increased indentation and often using smaller type

dust jacket (also **jacket**)
a removable paper cover, usually decorative, protecting a hardback book

ebook
> an electronic copy of a book that can be read by means of a PC or similar device

editing
> the process of preparing material for publication, including, where necessary, making corrections and suggesting other amendments

edition
> the entire number of copies of a publication issued at one time or from a single setting of type

em
> a measure of width used for type (equivalent to the width of a roman capital M in the typeface being used)

en
> a measure of width used for type that is half the size of an em

end matter (also **endlims**)
> pages that follow the main text in a book, including appendix, bibliography, index etc

endnote
> a note printed at the end of a book or chapter

endpapers
> leaves of paper pasted to the inside front and back of a hardback book's boards to secure the binding

epigraph
> a short quotation at the beginning of a book or chapter

errata slip
> a list of errors and their corrections inserted in a book after printing

face
> the front cover of a book; also used as an abbreviation for *typeface*

final read
> the last reading of a typeset proof for errors before it goes to the printer

flush
> text aligned with a straight edge to the left or right, as in *flush left, flush right* (see **justified setting**)

flyer
> a small handbill promoting a book

flyleaf
> a blank page at the beginning or end of a book

folio
> 1 the page number in a book *or* 2 an individual leaf of paper

font
> a complete set of characters of one size of the same typeface

footer
a line at the bottom of each page of a book containing, for example, the book or chapter title (see also **header** and **running head or foot**)

footnote
a note printed at the bottom of a page, usually in a smaller type size

foreword
a commendatory introduction at the beginning of a book, written by someone other than the author

format
the shape, size and binding of a book

frontispiece
an illustration placed opposite the title page of a book

genre
a particular style or type of writing, for example science fiction, romance, or mystery

glossary
an alphabetical list of terms and their definitions, usually relating to a specific subject or text

grid
a design technique used to determine the internal divisions of a page

gsm
the measurement of the weight of paper (grams per square metre)

gutter
the inside margin between facing pages of a book

half-title
the first page of a book, bearing only the title

hard copy
the printed-out version of a document

header
a line at the top of each page of a book containing, for example, the book or chapter title (see also **footer** and **running head or foot**)

heading
a title at the head of a page, chapter or section of a book

house style
the textual presentation (including spelling conventions etc) and general layout style preferred by a specific publisher

imprint
the name and address of a book's publisher and/or printer, usually given on the verso of the title page

index
an alphabetical list of names and/or subjects contained in a book, with references to the pages where they occur

ISBN (International Standard Book Number)
an international system by which each book title published is assigned a unique 13-digit number

ISSN (International Standard Serial Number)
an international system by which each journal title published is assigned a unique 8-digit number

kerning
adjusting the space between letters to avoid large gaps or squeezing

JPEG (Joint Photographic Experts Group)
a data file format used to store and display graphics and images digitally

justified setting
the process of adjusting the spacing between characters to ensure the even alignment of text against the book's right or left margins

lamination
a layer of protective plastic film covering a dust jacket, paperback cover or binding board

landscape
the shape of an illustration or book where the width is greater than the height (see also **portrait**)

layout
the design of a page showing the positioning of text and illustrations

leading
a measured blank space between lines of print

leaf
a single sheet of paper, forming two pages in a book

Legal Deposit
the requirement in law in the UK and Ireland for a publisher to donate one copy of each publication to the British Library and also if requested to the five other Legal Deposit libraries

libel
the publication of an untrue statement damaging to a person's reputation

limited edition
a publication which is produced in a specified small quantity and often numbered and signed by the author

lowercase
small letters such as *a, b, c*, as opposed to uppercase letters such as *A, B, C*

manuscript (MS)
a handwritten or typed text before it is typeset and printed (see also **typescript, TS**)

mark up
to annotate or amend a text in preparation for typesetting or printing

matt finish
a non-glossy cover finish

mock-up
a sample of what a page or book will look like when printed

opening
adjacent left-hand and right-hand pages, sometimes called a *spread*

orphan
the first line of a paragraph appearing on its own at the bottom of a page

pagination
page numbering

PDF (Portable Document Format)
a data file format that captures and sends an electronic document in exactly the format intended by the originator

perfect binding
a method of binding the pages of a book using adhesive (as opposed to sewing)

permission
authorisation to reproduce copyright material

plagiarism
copying another person's work without permission and passing it off as one's own

point size
height of a letter or character

portrait
the shape of an illustration or book where the height is greater than the width (see also **landscape**)

preface
an introductory note by the author at the beginning of a book

prelims
pages preceding the main text of a book, including half-title, title page, imprint page, contents list etc

print-on-demand
the means whereby copies of a book may be printed as and when required

print-ready copy
material that is supplied digitally to the printer as part of the book production process

print run
the number of copies of a book printed at the one time

proof
a photocopy provided by the typesetter or printer to allow for checking and correction in advance of a book going to press

proofreading
reading and, if necessary, correcting proofs provided by the typesetter or printer

publication date
> 1 the year in which a book is published *or* 2 the specific date on which a book is released for sale (e.g. 6 March 2008)

ragged
> text set with an uneven margin, as in *ragged right* and *ragged left* (see also **flush** and **justified setting**)

recto
> the right-hand page in a book, always an odd number

reissue
> to republish a book after it has been out of print for a period of time

remaindering
> selling off books at reduced prices to clear stock

reprint
> an uncorrected republication of a book, sometimes with a new title page, foreword or cover

returns
> unsold books that are sent back by a bookseller to the publisher (see also **sale-or-return** and **see-safe**)

review copy
> a complimentary copy of a book provided by the publisher in the hope of generating a review or notice

rough
> 1 a rough drawing by the author, or presented by an illustrator, that will need to be redrawn before presentation to the printer *or* 2 sample work presented by designer for approval

royalty
> an agreed percentage of the revenue made on the sale of a book to be paid to the author

running head or foot
> a repeated line of type, such as the book or chapter title, that appears at the top or bottom of every page

sale-or-return
> a system allowing booksellers not to pay for a consignment of books until they know how many they have sold (unsold books in sellable condition may be returned at this stage and their value deducted from the original invoice)

see-safe
> a system that requires a bookseller to pay the full invoice amount for a consignment of books within an agreed payment period, but which allows him or her to return unsold books in sellable condition at a later date in return for a credit note or repayment

serif/sans serif
> kinds of typeface: *serif* is slightly more formal and generally preferred by publishers when text is being typeset

small caps
small capital letters, often used for acronyms (e.g. UNESCO) and approximately the same size as a lowercase x in the same typeface

specification
detailed instructions regarding a proposed book, such as the number of pages, size, binding and schedule

spine
the part of the book that connects the front to the back and which can be seen when a book is upright on a shelf

spread
a pair of facing pages (left-hand and right-hand) that are treated as a single entity and designed together

style sheet
1 a list of variable spellings, capitalisations etc, made by the copy-editor for the attention of the typesetter and proofreader *or* 2 a set of style and typography guidelines issued by the publisher to the author, to ensure uniformity throughout the book

subsidiary right
the right to publish a book in ways other than its original form, for example as a paperback, a film or an audio book

title page
a page at the beginning of the book that lists the complete title of the work and the names of the author and publisher

typeface
the style and size of the type used in a document, for example Times New Roman, Arial etc, sometimes loosely referred to as the font (see also **font**)

typescript (TS)
a typed or word-processed version of a document

typesetting
arranging type or data in preparation for printing

typo
a typographical error

uppercase
large letters such as *A, B, C* as opposed to lowercase letters *a, b, c*

unjustified setting
text with ragged margins (see also **justified setting**)

verso
the left-hand page in a book, always an even number

widow
the last word or line of a paragraph when it appears on its own at the top of a page

Index

This book is printed on 150 gsm Satimatt paper. The main text is set 10 point on 12.5 leading in Adobe Garamond, with side panels set in Gill Sans and headings in Helvetica Neue.